Games, Ideas and Activities for
Primary Phonics

Games, Ideas and Activities for Primary Phonics

Gill Coulson and Lynn Cousins

PEARSON

Harlow, England • London • New York • Boston • San Francisco • Toronto • Sydney
Auckland • Singapore • Hong Kong • Tokyo • Seoul • Taipei • New Delhi
Cape Town • São Paulo • Mexico City • Madrid • Amsterdam • Munich • Paris • Milan

PEARSON EDUCATION LIMITED
Edinburgh Gate
Harlow CM20 2JE
United Kingdom
Tel: +44 (0)1279 623623
Fax: +44 (0)1279 431059
website: www.pearson.com/uk

First published in Great Britain in 2012

The rights of Gill Coulson and Lynn Cousins to be identified as authors of this work
have been asserted by them in accordance with the Copyright, Designs and Patents Act 1988.

ISBN: 978-1-4082-9205-1

British Library Cataloguing-in-Publication Data
A catalogue record for this book is available from the British Library

Library of Congress Cataloging-in-Publication Data
Coulson, Gill.
   Games, ideas and activities for primary phonics / Gill Coulson and Lynn Cousins. -- 1st ed.
      p. cm.
   Includes bibliographical references.
   ISBN 978-1-4082-9205-1
   1. Reading--Phonetic method--Activity programs. 2. Reading--Phonetic method--Study and teaching
(Primary) I. Cousins, Lynn. II. Title.

   LB1050.34.C68 2012
   372.46'5--dc23

                         2011050348

10 9 8 7 6 5 4 3 2 1
16 15 14 13 12

Cartoon illustrations by Cathy Hughes
Typeset in 8.5 News Gothic BT by 30
Printed and bound in Malaysia (CTP-VP)

With thanks to John and Tim

Contents

Introduction

Making the teaching of phonics interesting for the children is a daily challenge for teachers. *Primary Phonics* is a resource for those who want to make their teaching of phonics fun and dynamic, and who want their children to develop the confidence to handle English spelling with all its variations.

It aims to:

- help you reinforce your phonics teaching in a fun way across the wider curriculum
- show you how to build phonic activities around the things that are already happening in your classroom
- demonstrate how you can take inspiration from published books, both fiction and non-fiction, new titles and familiar ones
- provide you with ideas for creating displays that link phonics with the rest of the curriculum
- encourage the children to play with words, increase their vocabulary and enjoy the idiosyncrasies of the English language.

The activities in *Primary Phonics* are all designed to reinforce and supplement your regular discrete phonics teaching. They will form links between phonics and other areas of the curriculum. As Ofsted inspectors wrote in their report, *Reading by Six. How the best schools do it.* (November 2010):

> *The best phonics teaching is characterised by ... reinforcement ... and active participation by all children.*

> (Taken from the summary of the report)

Primary Phonics is divided into three parts:

- *Using books*: taking inspiration from stories, poems and non-fiction reading. We are passionate about using texts that involve and motivate children, but feel that it's important to remember that the books should always be enjoyed as the authors intended.
- *Illustrating phonics*: using creative activities as a link to reinforce phonics. Each of the ideas easily adapts to small- or large-scale classroom displays or individual pieces of work in children's own workbooks.
- *Exploring sounds*: involving activities that contain a practical or investigative approach. We want to encourage children to have fun as they learn.

We have divided the activities into four incremental stages, each describing the way that children progress through their learning of synthetic phonics. Each activity clearly states which of the four stages it is most suited to.

A. Children who are practising their single-letter sounds. This includes any letter of the alphabet.
B. Children who are learning graphemes with more than one letter. This includes any group of letters that make up a single phoneme, but only one of the possible graphemes for that sound is included in each activity.
C. Children who are learning alternative graphemes. These activities each include one phoneme and some or all of its graphemes, or some graphemes and their various pronunciations.
D. Children who are gaining confidence with spelling. These activities may include more than one phoneme per activity, as well as prefixes, suffixes, tenses and plurals. They are intended for older or more able children.

We include tricky words, invented spellings and oral blending and segmenting as appropriate to each stage.

For ease of use the activities are grouped into these stages but are not incremental within that stage, e.g. the second activity isn't necessarily harder than the first.

Using the book

- Phonemes are the individual sounds that make up a language. We have used the symbols and letter groups as in *Letters and Sounds*. So a phoneme is written as, e.g., /a/ or /igh/.
- Graphemes are the written forms of those sounds. Following the style of *Letters and Sounds*, we have used, e.g., '**m**' or '**ch**'.
- We have given you lots of examples of responses that you or the children could use. All of these suggested ideas are in italics.
- When you need to sound out or segment a word we have used the style, e.g., m-ou-se.

The page layout has clear headings and is user-friendly.

Title: where we have based the activity around a book or a poem, this is used as the title.

A 'paper-clipped' note: this appears underneath the title and briefly describes the type of activity.

Suitable for: this refers to the incremental stages we have described.

Aims: this states which specific phoneme, grapheme, prefix, etc. is the focus of the activity. More information on this is given in the index of activities at the back of the book.

Resources: where these are needed they are listed here, including the full book references.

What to do: step-by-step instructions along with lots of additional ideas, suggested responses and examples.

Variations: some of these are complete activities, others are amendments to the content or the outcome of the original activity.

Cross-curricular links: each activity is linked to another aspect of Key Stage One of the curriculum so that you can include phonics teaching at different times throughout the day.

Phonics is a means to an end. Practitioners and teachers must bear in mind that ... children need to understand the purpose of learning phonics and have lots of opportunities to apply their developing skills in interesting and engaging reading and writing activities.

(Letters and Sounds: Notes of Guidance for Practitioners and Teachers, p.3)

About the authors

Gill Coulson and Lynn Cousins are on a mission to convince teachers and children that phonics can be fun!

They have both worked extensively in the Early Years and Key Stage One. Gill was a deputy head and a tutor for initial training, and Lynn was a head teacher. Throughout their teaching careers they continued to study: Gill gained an M.Phil. degree, researching the teaching of reading, and Lynn gained an MA(Ed.) in Early Years' education. Gill has taught focused writing groups in local schools and Lynn has been an editor of educational publications. She has written a number of published books, including *Shaping Children's Behaviour in the Early Years* for the Essential Guides series.

Gill and Lynn have also written *Early Years Phonics* and *Early Years Literacy* in the Classroom Gems series. The authors present workshops that show practitioners and teachers how to bring interactive phonics into every part of the curriculum.

Acknowledgements

With thanks to the authors and illustrators, the poets and the artists who continue to inspire us.

Part 1
Using books

Chapter 1
Stage A

Monkey and Me

Play a miming game based on the descriptive words you have collected.

Suitable for

Children who are practising single-letter sounds.

Aims

To remind the children of the phoneme /m/.

Resources

- Gravett, E. (2008) *Monkey and Me*, London: Macmillan's Children's Books

What to do

- After enjoying the story, ask the children what sort of monkey was the one in the book.
  Other monkeys might behave in different ways. Can the children suggest any?
  Children could demonstrate their ideas by actions, mimes or making voice sounds.
- After a few suggestions, ask them to concentrate on words that begin with /m/, the same as 'monkey'.
  Now what words can they think of?
- Children can now work in pairs to think of a descriptive word for the monkey and work out how they could show it. They take it in turns to show their idea. Can the other children guess their word?

Here are some ideas:
- *musical monkey*
- *mad monkey*
- *miserable monkey*
- *magic monkey*
- *mini-monkey*
- *mischievous monkey*
- *messy monkey*
- *mysterious monkey*

Variation

- Use one of the other animals that feature in the story.

Cross-curricular link

PSHE: to play cooperatively with others.

Nursery rhymes

Practise the vowel sounds as you adapt a nursery rhyme.

Suitable for

Children who are practising single-letter sounds.

Aims

To encourage the children to focus on the medial vowel sounds as they blend and segment words.

Resources

- A copy of the rhyme 'To market, to market, to buy a fat pig'
- Some CVC (consonant-vowel-consonant) words written on individual cards in a box or basket – start with pig, peg, pug

What to do

- Place the two cards, *peg* and *pug* in the box. Sit in a circle with the box near you.
- Say the rhyme with the children, encouraging them to join in:

    To market, to market, to buy a fat pig
    Home again, home again, jiggety jig

- Ask the children to listen carefully to the last word on each line. Do they notice that they are rhyming words?
  Say the individual sounds of the word 'pig', /p/ /i/ /g/, and then of 'jig', /j/ /i/ /g/.
- Choose a child to reach into the box and take out a card. They should then read it to the rest of the group, e.g., *peg*.

- Say the rhyme again, saying 'peg' instead of 'pig'. What happens to the rhyme when you do this? They will have to change 'jig' as well. Who can tell you what it will be? Say the rhyme with both words changed:

  To market, to market, to buy a fat peg
  Home again, home again, jiggety jeg

- Add the card with 'pig' on it to the box and start again, with a child choosing a card and then everyone trying to work out what it says, and what it will rhyme with so that you can all say the rhyme again.
- You could add some other CVC words to the box: e.g., *dog, hog, log, wig, fig, rug, mug*.

Variation

- Instead of reading the card chosen from the box, ask the children to segment the word and the others in the group can blend it to find out what it is.

Cross-curricular link

English: identifying patterns of rhyme.

The Tiger who Came to Tea (1)

Make up a new story with other animals that might come to tea.

Suitable for

Children who are practising single-letter sounds.

Aims

To help children use and recognise the phoneme /t/.

Resources

- Kerr, J. (1973) *The Tiger who Came to Tea*, London: Collins Picture Lions

What to do

- After enjoying the story, tell the children you are going to make a new story.
  Ask them to guess what animal is ringing the doorbell in this story. After listening to a few suggestions, explain that only animals with names that begin with the same sound as tiger can come to tea. How many other animals can the children name that start with /t/?
- You may want to write down their suggestions on pieces of card for them to hold or you may prefer that this is a purely verbal activity.
- Briefly retell the beginning of the story where Sophie opens the door. *'And there was a t ...'*
  Encourage the first child to provide a suggestion, then invite another child to make a guess by saying:
  'or it could have been a t ...'
- Continue with several animals that begin with /t/. A discussion might follow on what constitutes an 'animal'. Are birds, fish and insects included in your list? Are prehistoric animals allowed?

Here are some ideas:

> *tortoise, turtle, tadpole, toad, turkey, tawny owl, tyrannosaurus rex, triceratops, trout, tiddler, termite, tiger moth*

- Choose one animal to continue with the story,
  'Yes, it was a t ...'

Variation

- Let the children choose an animal and make their own version of the book. They might like to personalise the story further by using their own name. When they make their cover, take the time to look at the cover of the story-book and notice the use of both the capital letter and the small-case 't'.

Cross-curricular link

English: reading.

The Tiger who Came to Tea (2)

> What can we make for the tiger's tea? He only likes to eat food that begins with /t/.

Suitable for

Children who are practising single-letter sounds.

Aims

To help children use and remember the phoneme /t/.

Resources

- Kerr, J. (1973) *The Tiger who Came to Tea*, London: Collins Picture Lions

What to do

- After enjoying the story, tell the children that maybe the tiger ate all that food because he couldn't find what he really likes. Maybe tigers only like food that begins with the same sound as their name!
- Ask the children questions to assess their understanding, e.g.
  - 'Do tigers like sausages?'
  - 'Do they like cheese?'
  - 'Do they like trifle?' – Yes!
- Can they suggest any food that tigers would like?
  Here are some ideas:

  teacakes, tikka massala, tortilla, tarts, tomatoes, tomato soup, turnips, tuna sandwiches, trifle, tiramisu, toffee, tandoori chicken, thyme, trout, turkey, taramasalata

Variation

- For children at a more advanced level. Ask the children to listen carefully.

  When the tiger comes for tea,
  We can have toast – but not bread
  We can have tea – but not coffee
  We can have tangerines – but not oranges

Can any of the children make up sentences following this pattern you have given them? It is more difficult because they have to recall a food beginning with /t/ and then compare it with something similar that he won't eat.

Cross-curricular link

English: responding to stories.

Not Now, Bernard

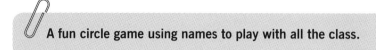

A fun circle game using names to play with all the class.

Suitable for

Children who are practising single-letter sounds.

Aims

To help children use and remember the phoneme /n/.

Resources

- McKee, D. (1990) *Not Now, Bernard*, London: Red Fox, Random House Children's Books

What to do

- Read and enjoy the book together. Then ask the children to sit in a circle for a game. Explain that everyone can choose someone else's name then have a turn to say 'Not now ...' using the name of their choice.
- The teacher starts the game by saying 'Not now, Susie', using the name of a child in the circle. Susie then has her turn and uses the name of another child in the class. Keep going until everyone has had a turn.
- Explain to the children that *not* and *now* begin with the same sound. Is there someone in the class with a name beginning with /n/? Ask the children to think of other names beginning with /n/. You might include:

    Norman, Noah, Nisha, Natalie, Niamh, Nancy, Nicholas, Neil, Nathan, Noel, Nicola, Natasha, Naomi, Nadia

- Now tell the children that this time they can make up names. The teacher starts by repeating 'Not now …' and using any new name, e.g. Angie. Continue round the circle letting the children take turns to repeat the sentence with different names. If someone gives a name that begins with /n/, ask them to stand up and everyone should give them a clap. This child remains standing as the game continues round the circle.
- When a second child suggests a name beginning with /n/ they also stand and everyone gives them a clap. Then the two children can change places and sit down.
- Continue the game in this way. The more children who suggest names beginning with /n/ the more fun there will be!

Variation

- One child can be in the centre of the circle doing a mime of a simple action, e.g. Mum watering the plants. The other children can take it in turns to guess the mime. If they are wrong the child replies 'Not now, Bernard', but if they guess correctly they swap places and that child can then have a turn at miming an action.

Cross-curricular link

PSHE: to play cooperatively with others.

Five Minutes' Peace

After enjoying the story, spend some time thinking about peaceful places.

Suitable for

Children who are practising single-letter sounds.

Aims

To help children use the phoneme /p/.

Resources

- Murphy, J. (1998) *Five Minutes' Peace*, London: Walker Books Ltd

---

What to do

- Enjoy the book together then look again at the title.
- Do the children understand the word – peace?
  Encourage several children to describe the meaning.
  Can they suggest any peaceful places?
- Now tell the children you are going to think of places that begin with /p/.

These might include:

> palace, pancake parlour, pantomime, park, party, peace
> pergola, pebbly beach, petrol station, piano concert, pig sty,
> pizza restaurant, playground, police station, pond, puppet
> show, pushchair

- As the children make their suggestions, write them on pieces of card.
- Now you are going to sort them into peaceful places and not peaceful places.
  Write these two titles on the board.

> • Sort all the places you have thought of that begin with /p/. This
>   will promote discussion amongst the children as they realise that
>   sometimes the places are peaceful, and sometimes they are not.

Variations

- Discuss with the children when they enjoy some peace.
  Ask the children to complete this sentence-starter:
  'I have five minutes' peace ....'
  They might suggest:
  - at bedtime
  - when I'm thinking
  - when I'm doing school work
  - when I'm talking with a friend
  - having a cuddle with Mummy or Daddy
  - listening to stories
  - watching television
  - during assembly time.
  Discuss why it's important to have some quiet times.
- Tell the children that the musical symbol for playing quietly is /p/.
  Hold up the letter /p/ and tell the children this is the signal for quiet time.
  Let the children chatter to their friends but explain that when you hold up the
  /p/ they must stop talking and all sit quietly.
  Now everyone can enjoy a few moments' peace – you probably won't manage
  five minutes!
  Keep the card – you never know when it might be useful.

Cross-curricular link

RE: opportunities for meditation and quiet thought.

The Very Lazy Ladybird

After enjoying the book, think of some new alliterative titles.

Suitable for

Children who are practising single-letter sounds.

Aims

To help children recognise and use the phoneme /l/ and practise the tricky word **the**.

Resources

- Finn, I. and Tickle, J. (2000) *The Very Lazy Ladybird*, London: Little Tiger Press

What to do

- Read the title to the children, pointing to each word on the front of the book.
  Ask who can read the first word of the title? **The**.
- Write the word on the board.
  Now ask them to look closely at the order of the three letters.
- Explain to the children that the 'T' is written with a capital letter because it's in the title. Remind the children how to write the small case 't', if appropriate.
- Cover the word on the board and ask if anyone can point to it on the book.
  'Well done!'
- Ask the children what sound 'ladybird' begins with.
  Read the title and ask if they can hear another word beginning with that same sound.

- Explain that this story is about a lazy ladybird – both words begin with the same sound but can anyone think of a new title? Remember to use a word beginning with /l/.
  See how many new story titles you can think of: The Very L... Ladybird.
- Ideas might include:

  long, late, light, lovely, lilac, large, lively, lonely, last, lost, likeable, loud, lucky, little

- The children might like to talk about what would happen to the ladybird in their new stories.

Variation

- Children could design a book cover for their story idea or use one of their ideas for a shared writing activity.

Cross-curricular link

Science: mini-beasts.

Kipper's Birthday

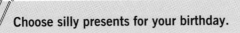

Choose silly presents for your birthday.

Suitable for

Children who are practising single-letter sounds.

Aims

To help children focus on the /i/ medial vowel sound.

Resources

- Inkpen, M. (2011) *Kipper's Birthday and other stories*, London: Hachette Children's Books
- Two boxes
- Words on individual cards. On one colour of card write: *pink, silver, wicked, singing, thin, silly, big*. On a second colour card write: *pig, ring, wig, fish, pin, bin, lid*

What to do

- Working with a small group of children, read all of the cards together. Encourage the children to notice that they each have the /i/ grapheme.
- Explain to them that one set are all the names of things – you may choose to use the term 'nouns'.
  The other group of cards are all words that tell you what things are like, they describe things – or use the term 'adjectives'.
- Put the cards into two boxes, one for each colour.
- Choose one child to be the birthday boy or girl. This child chooses two friends. These two children are each going to pick a card at random – without looking! One child will pick a noun, and the other will be picking an adjective.

- Hand these to the birthday child who will read them to find out what present they have. Make this as much fun as you can, reminding the children that they are meant to be funny presents, e.g., *a singing wig*.
- Return the cards to the boxes so that there is always an interesting selection of possible presents. Then choose another child to have a birthday.
- Continue in this way until everyone has had a chance to be the birthday child, and hopefully everyone has had a turn at picking a card.

Variation

- Children can record their own silly birthday present list by picking out two random cards and writing them down. Keep returning the cards to the boxes. Children can write and draw as many presents as they wish.

Cross-curricular link

PSHE: special days.

Nursery rhyme quiz

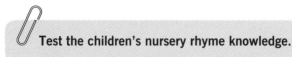

Test the children's nursery rhyme knowledge.

Suitable for

Children who are practising single-letter sounds.

Aims

To encourage the children to think about names and words that contain the phoneme /o/.

Resources

- A selection of nursery rhyme books

What to do

- Sit round a table with a small group of children. Put a selection of nursery rhyme books with illustrations on the table.
- Tell the children that you are going to ask them some questions about characters and events in nursery rhymes, and they should try to think of the answer.
- Explain to them that every answer will have an /o/ sound in it. They can look through the books if they can't think of the answer straight away.
- Here are some ideas for questions:
    Who had a dolly that was sick? Miss Polly
    Which creatures sat on a speckled log? Frogs
    What did a mouse run up? A clock
    Who had to put the kettle on? Polly
    Who lost her pocket? Lucy Locket
    What happened to the sausages in the pan? They went 'pop'
    What was short and stout? The little teapot
    Who was the piper's son? Tom

> *What sort of pet did old Mother Hubbard have? A dog*
> *Who went to Gloucester in a shower of rain? Doctor Foster*
> *Which buns cost one a penny or two a penny? Hot cross buns*

Variation

- More able children could choose their favourite of these rhymes to copy out and illustrate.

Cross-curricular link

English: nursery rhymes.

The Tale of Mrs Tiggy·Winkle

Find some alliterative connections with your hedgehog's job.

Suitable for

Children who are practising single-letter sounds.

Aims

To help children practise using picture dictionaries to look for words that start with /h/.

Resources

- Potter, B. (1987) *The Tale of Mrs Tiggy-Winkle*. London: Frederick Warne
- Picture dictionaries
- Narrow strips of paper, brown felt-tip pens and glue

What to do

- Read the book with the children and enjoy looking at the pictures of hedgehogs.
- Who can tell you what job Mrs Tiggy-Winkle does? 'She's a washerwoman.' What would she actually do? What sort of things do you see her washing in the book?
- Can any of the children tell you other jobs that characters – or hedgehogs – might do? Collect as many as you can. Take some of the children's suggestions and ask for words that would describe some of the things that they might do, or deal with, e.g.
  - *Hairdresser: hair, shampoo, combs, hairdryers*
  - *Policeman: traffic, robbers, sirens, fast cars*
- Now ask the children to tell you what sound 'hedgehog' begins with/: /h/.

- What if the hedgehog was a gardener? Can they think of anything that they might do or use – BUT it has to begin with /h/ just like 'hedgehog'. They might suggest: *holly, hoe, hyacinth, heather, herbs*. As they suggest ideas, show them how you can write each one on a strip of paper using a brown felt pen.
- Now draw a simple hedgehog shape and give it an eye and a smile. Stick your strips of paper, with the words written on them, onto the drawing to look like the hedgehog's spines.
- The children can work in pairs to make their own hedgehog. What job will theirs do? You could tell each pair a job, e.g. *vet, chef, teacher, doctor, clothes-shop assistant*.

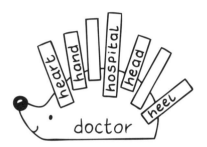

- They can use the picture dictionaries to find some words that begin with /h/ that are connected with that job, e.g.,
  - *Vet: horse, hippo, hog, hyena, hen*
  - *Chef: hot dog, ham, hula-hoops, haggis, honey*
  - *Teacher: Harry, Harvey, Helen, Hannah, Henry*
  - *Doctor: head, hand, hospital, heart, heel*
  - *Clothes-shop assistant: hat, headband, helmet, handbag, hood*
- When all the hedgehogs are finished they could be used as a small display with the title 'Can you guess what we do?'. Or the children could write their own label: 'This hedgehog is a doctor', etc.

Variation

- Children could work independently to make a little family of hedgehogs, each with their own job. Make the spines in the same way.

Cross-curricular link

PSHE: people and their roles in life.

Under my umbrella

An accumulative reading game to play when you are doing work on weather.

Suitable for

Children who are practising single-letter sounds.

Aims

To focus the children's attention on the grapheme /u/ when reading.

Resources

- Any books on umbrellas or weather. Try:
- Allen, P. (2009) *Grandpa and Thomas and the Green Umbrella*, London: Penguin/Puffin Books
- Individual cards of CVC words with a medial /u/ vowel, e.g., *cup*, *fun*, *tub*, *mug*, *gun*, *run*, *sun*, *but*, *cut*, *put*, *nut*, *bug*, *dug*, *hug*, *rub*, *rug*
- Blu-Tack

What to do

- Sit in a circle with the children.
- Children may be familiar with the memory game 'In my basket I have ...'. Remind them of this, and explain that this time they are going to read rather than remember words.
- Show them the words that you have already prepared. Read them through together. Do they notice that every word has the same middle letter? Can they tell you its name and the sound it makes in these words?
- Spread the cards out so that they can all be seen. Have some Blu-Tack ready.

- Start the game by saying the words, *'Under my umbrella I have ...'*. Now you choose one of the cards, e.g., *sun*, say it out loud and stick it at the top of the whiteboard.
- The next child in the circle says the words, *'Under my umbrella I have a sun and ...'*. They now choose a card, say it out loud and stick it underneath your card on the whiteboard. Continue in this way as long as interest holds.

Variation

- Once the children are familiar with lots of /u/ words they could play this in the traditional way as a memory game.

Cross-curricular link

Science: weather.

Avocado Baby

A book to interest children in avocados and the phoneme /a/.

Suitable for

Children who are practising single-letter sounds.

Aims

To give children practice identifying and using the phoneme /a/.

Resources

- Burningham, J. (1994) *Avocado Baby*, London: Red Fox, Random House Children's Books
- A baby doll
- Music or an instrument to play

What to do

- Enjoy the book together.
- Discuss why the baby is called the avocado baby.
  Has anyone tasted an avocado?
- Ask what sound avocado begins with. Can anyone think of another word beginning with the same sound?
- Collect a few suggestions from the children, e.g. *apple, ant, alligator, animal, ambulance, ankle, anorak, asparagus, America.*
- Show the children the baby doll and tell them you are going to play a game.
- Remind the children that in the story the baby likes avocados and tell the children they need to say something else that begins with /a/ that the baby might like, e.g. 'The baby likes avocados and ants'.
  (It might be appropriate to prepare the children further by saying the sentence a few times yourself using different examples.)

- Sit in a circle and explain that you are going to play some music while the baby is passed gently around the circle from child to child.
- When the music stops the child holding the baby doll says, 'The baby likes avocados and ...', choosing something else to add that begins with the phoneme /a/.
- If the child holding the baby struggles to think of an appropriate word, encourage other children to help with ideas.
- When the music continues the baby is passed around again until the music stops and a different child holding the baby must try to think of something for their sentence,
  e.g. *The baby likes avocados and ... animals.*

Variation

- You could also include children's names beginning with the phoneme /a/, e.g. *Abdul, Adam, Agnes, Alex, Alan, Alison, Anna, Andrew.* Encourage the children to think of the names before the game begins.

Cross-curricular link

PSHE: likes and dislikes.

Search the library

Make a class list of books with alliterative titles.

Suitable for

Children who are practising single-letter sounds.

Aims

To encourage children to notice the use of letters and sounds around them as they look carefully at book titles.

Resources

- Access to the school library
- A large sheet of paper labelled 'Do you notice anything?'
- A selection of books, most of them with alliterative titles

What to do

- Have your selection of books ready to show the children.
- Hold up one of the books that has an alliterative title and ask the children if anyone can tell you what it is called. Help them to read it if necessary.
- Now hold up a second book with an alliterative title and again ask the children to read the title. Ask them if they noticed anything special about the titles of these two books. You may need to direct their thinking to help them to notice eventually that each word in the title begins with the same letter.
- Show the children the paper and read the label on it together. Then choose two children to write the titles to these books in a list on the paper. Remind them to write them one underneath the other.
- Look at the other books you have chosen. Some of them have titles where all the words start with the same letter. Can the children identify them? If so, they should add them to your list.

- Over the day children can go in pairs to the library and each child can try to find one more title to go on your list.
  How many do the children think they can find altogether?
- In a very short time we found, *Worst Witch*, *Horrible Histories*, *Horrid Henry*, *Mucky Mabel* and *Naughty Nancy*!

Variations

- Children could paint pictures of the named alliterative characters and label them for a display.
- Use this as an opportunity to talk about capital letters for titles.

Cross-curricular link

English: characters in stories.

Little Bear Lost

> Play a game where children indicate thumbs up or down to show if the correct initial sound has been used.

Suitable for

Children who are practising single-letter sounds.

Aims

To help children use and identify the phoneme /b/.

Resources

- Hissey, J. (1995) *Little Bear Lost*, London: Hutchinson Children's Books
- Small toy bear to pass around the circle

What to do

- Read and enjoy the book together. Show them your toy bear. Let the children tell you about their special toy bears.
- Sit in a circle and write the word 'bear' for the children. Ask them to read the word and identify the initial sound.
- Explain to the children they are going to complete the sentence: 'The bear saw a...' with a word that begins with the sound /b/.
- If they are right everyone will give them the thumbs up sign, but if they are wrong they will get a thumbs down sign.
- Give the children an example: *The bear saw a bed.*
  Ask them to give you the thumbs up sign if they think it's correct.
- Then give them another example: *The bear saw a balloon.*
- Ask them to show you with their thumb sign if that's correct or not. It might be appropriate to collect together nouns beginning with /b/ before you begin the game. Suggestions might include: *baby, banana, bag, ball, banjo, bath, bell, bird, biscuit, boat, book, box, boy, bridge, bucket, bus, butterfly.*

- Give the toy bear to the first child and ask them to complete the sentence.
  Let the rest of the children respond with their thumb signs before the toy is handed on to the next child to take a turn.
- Encourage the use of adjectives beginning with /b/ to extend the range of items that can be listed, e.g., *blue*, *brown*, *black*, *big*, *baggy*, *bendy*, *best*, *beautiful*, *bright*.
- You could use this activity to assess the children's ability to hear and use the phoneme /b/.

Variation

- You can play this game with any other initial letter with a soft toy beginning with that sound. To make the game more difficult you could use two sounds that the children find hard to differentiate, e.g., /b/ and /p/. The children would get a thumbs up for: *The bear saw a bed,* or for *The pig saw a peg*; and a thumbs down for: *The bear saw a peg.*

Cross-curricular link

Science: living things.

'Round and round the garden'

Have some fun with these rhymes about Granny and her garden.

Suitable for

Children who are practising single-letter sounds.

Aims

To focus the children's attention on the /g/ phoneme.

Resources

- Outdoor space and skipping ropes or balls

What to do

- Sit together and remind the children of the rhyme: Round and round the garden/Goes the teddy bear, etc. Tell them that today they are going to learn a new rhyme (or two) about a garden, but this time it's not a teddy bear in the garden, but Granny.
- Before using these rhymes spend some time collecting together the children's suggestions for words beginning with /g/, e.g., *goat, ghost, glove, goose, gown, guitar, goggles, garage, gifts.*
- Now can they think of any names beginning with /g/? e.g., *Gary, Graham, Gretel, Grace, Gus, Grandad.*
- The first rhyme can be repeated by the children as they skip or as they bounce a ball. Try to keep the rhythm going.

     Granny's in the garden,
     Granny shuts the gate,
     Granny has to be in bed by half-past eight.

- Do it again, but this time change the word 'Granny' for other names that start with the /g/ phoneme.
- Sit together in a circle. Say the second rhyme with the children.

    In my granny's garden,
    Down by the gate,
    There's a great big goose
    Sitting on a plate.

- Remind the children of the words beginning with /g/.
- Now, say the rhyme again and each time you say it point to a child to suggest a /g/ word to fit at the end of line three.

Variation

- Children could write and illustrate their own version of either rhyme.

Cross-curricular link

English: rhythm and rhyme.

Chapter 2
Stage B

Brown Bear, Brown Bear, What Can You See?

Use this familiar book to encourage oral blending and segmenting.

Suitable for

Children who are learning graphemes of more than one letter.

Aims

To help children learn the skills of oral blending and segmenting.

Resources

- Martin, J. and Carle, E. (1986) *Brown Bear, Brown Bear, What Can You See?*, London: Picture Lions
- A list of the animals in the book for your use

What to do

- Sit in a circle and after enjoying the book together put the book in the centre.
- Tell the children you are going to play a guessing game. Can they work out which animal you are remembering?
- Segment the colour and name of the animal.
  I can remember a b-l-ue h-or-se.
- Ask the children to raise their hands if they know which animal you remember from the story.
- The child who gives the right answer can go to the book and open at the page showing the animal mentioned before returning to their place.
- Continue with the ten animals featured in the story.

Variation

- Ask the children who answered correctly to segment the coloured animal they identified. Then other children have a second attempt to recognise them using oral blending.

Cross-curricular link

Science: animals.

The Blue Balloon

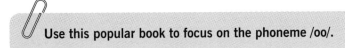

Use this popular book to focus on the phoneme /oo/.

Suitable for

Children who are learning graphemes of more than one letter.

Aims

To help children recognise the phoneme /oo/.

Resources

- Inkpen, M. (1991) *The Blue Balloon*, Sevenoaks, Kent: Picture Knight Edition: Hodder and Stoughton Children's Books
- Lots of small pieces of paper with an individual letter printed on each piece – you will need several copies of c, d, f, l, m, n, p, r, s, t, z
- Print the letters 'oo' on several other small pieces of paper

What to do

- Enjoy the book with a small group.
- Then look at the title of the book. Who can point to the word 'balloon'?
- Segment the word into phonemes, explaining that there are two letters 'l' for the /l/ sound.
- Point to the double 'o' and ask if anyone knows what this sound is – /oo/.
- Can the children think of any other words with /oo/?
  Accept all suggestions that have the /oo/ phoneme even if they are spelt differently.
- If you want to use this opportunity to introduce an alternative grapheme to the children, then segment the word 'blue' in the title to demonstrate another spelling of the /oo/ phoneme.
- Show the children the cards with the 'oo' written on them.

- Ask them to use these with the letter cards to create words with the phoneme /oo/.
  Use these letters – c, d, f, l, m, n, p, r, s, t, z – with /oo/ to create a range of words, e.g. *food*, *mood*, *tool*, *fool*, *cool*, *stool*, *spoon*, *moon*, *zoo*.
- Now the children can record the words they've made by gluing the letters onto a blue balloon shape.

Variation

- The children could produce as many words as they can while you blow up a balloon!

Cross-curricular link

English: responding to literature.

'Flo's Toe'

Use this amusing poem to stimulate interest in rhyming words.

Suitable for

Children who are learning graphemes of more than one letter.

Aims

To develop children's awareness of graphemes of more than one letter.

Resources

- Foster, J. (chosen by) (2003) *Completely Crazy Poems*, London: Collins, imprint of HarperCollins

What to do

- Read the poem 'Flo's Toe' by Trevor Harvey.
- When the children have enjoyed the poem, write out the poem on a whiteboard as the children identify the pairs of words that rhyme in this poem:
  - *Flo* and *toe*
  - *gloom* and *room*
  - *fright* and *right*
- Segment the words into their phonemes and encourage the children to notice how these are written.
- In the poem, *Flo* and *toe* do not share the same spelling of the grapheme /oa/ and the children may notice this and comment on it. Suggest changing the name to Uncle Joe instead.
- Rub out the name of *Auntie Flo* and replace it with *Uncle Joe*. Explain that as *Joe* and *toe* rhyme the next line of the poem doesn't need changing.

- Ask the children if they can suggest a different name for an auntie or an uncle that rhymes with something that can be used in a different version of the poem.
  Ideas might include:
    Ben and *hen*
    Rose and *nose*
    Ted and *bed*
    Lee and *knee*
- Try fitting their suggestions into the poem's structure verbally then ask the children to write out their own version of the poem.
- The children might enjoy illustrating one of the poems.

Variation

- Some of their suggestions may include alternative graphemes, e.g.
    Fred and *head*
    Paul and *wall*
    Bee and *flea*
    Burt and *shirt*

  This provides an opportunity for more able children to learn about some alternative graphemes in a meaningful context.

Cross-curricular link

English: poetry.

Frog is Frog

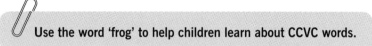

Use the word 'frog' to help children learn about CCVC words.

Suitable for

Children who are learning graphemes of more than one letter.

Aims

To help children use segmenting and oral blending skills to spell words with initial consonant blends.

Resources

- Velthuijs, M. (2005) *Frog is Frog*, London: Anderson Press Ltd

What to do

- Read and enjoy the book together.
- Read the title again then write *fog* on the board.
- Ask the children if the word is 'frog'.
- Encourage them to segment the word 'fog'.
  Who can explain what missing letter needs adding to make the word 'frog'?
- Write *frog* on the board as the children segment it into 4 phonemes.
- Write another word on the board that can be changed by adding the letter 'r', e.g. *dip*.
- Read the word together then ask how it can be changed to 'drip'.
  Decide together where the letter 'r' needs to be.
- Ask the children to write the new word on their whiteboards.
- Repeat with several other words, e.g. *fed, fill, tap, pint, tuck, cop, bag, cash, gasp, camp*.

Variation

- More able children could be challenged with words beginning with 's' that can be changed by adding l, n, p or t after the initial letter:

sap – snap

sank – spank

sell – spell

sick – stick

sand – stand

sing – sting

sack – snack

sit – slit

sap – slap

sip – slip

Cross·curricular link

English: words with common spelling patterns.

The Elephant and the Bad Baby

Write sentences about this accumulative story and help the children learn the grapheme 'ph'.

Suitable for

Children who are learning graphemes of more than one letter.

Aims

To provide an opportunity for children to read and write the grapheme 'ph'.

Resources

- Vipont, E. (2000) *The Elephant and the Bad Baby*, London: Picture Puffin
- Seven strips of card with a shopkeeper from the book printed on each one: e.g. The ice-cream man
- Another set of blank strips of card – the children will write on these to complete the sentence

What to do

- Read and enjoy the story, encouraging the children to join in.
  Did anyone guess why the baby was a bad baby?
- See if the children can remember all the shopkeepers in the order they run after the elephant.
  Show the card with that shopkeeper's name as the children mention them.
- Stick one card on the board and tell the children you want to write the rest of the sentence, e.g. 'The ice-cream man ... ran after the elephant'.
- Ask the children to segment the word 'elephant' as you write.
  (It might be appropriate to misspell it and write 'f' in the word, then ask the children to check with the title to see if it's correct.)

- Explain that in the word *elephant* the phoneme /f/ is written with 'ph'. (If you are lucky enough to have a child called Phillippa, Philip or Phoebe in your class you can illustrate another familiar example with their name card.)
- Give out the blank strips of card and ask the children to write the sentence endings on the cards, i.e. 'ran after the elephant'.
- Put the shopkeeper names in the centre of the table and let the children take turns to pick one up and fit it with their ending to create a sentence, e.g. 'The snack-bar man ran after the elephant'.
- Encourage the children to read their sentences aloud. They can then exchange the shopkeeper names to make a different sentence with their ending.
- The children might enjoy writing out their sentences and illustrating all the characters running after the elephant.

Variation

- More able children could be challenged to find other words with the 'ph' grapheme, e.g. *telephone, dolphin, nephew, photograph, alphabet.*

Cross-curricular link

English: responding to literature.

Knock, Knock. Who's There?

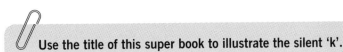

Use the title of this super book to illustrate the silent 'k'.

Suitable for

Children who are learning graphemes of more than one letter.

Aims

To introduce children to familiar words that start with the grapheme 'kn'.

Resources

• Browne, A. (2010) *Knock, Knock. Who's There?* London: Picture Puffin

What to do

• Read and enjoy the book together.
• Remind the children of the title of the book.
• Show the front cover and ask who can show you the words 'knock, knock'.
• Ask who notices something funny about the words 'knock, knock'. *The letter 'k' is not sounded.*
• Explain that 'k' is a silent letter, so although it comes before the letter 'n' all we say is the phoneme /n/.
• Ask for some words that begin with /n/ until you have collected a few other examples, e.g. *knife, knight, knee, knob, knuckle, know, knit, knot.*
   (If appropriate, discuss homophones, i.e. words that sound the same but are spelt differently for different meanings. E.g. *knight – night/knot – not/know – no.*)
• The children might be interested to know that many years ago people pronounced the letter 'k' in *knight*, for example, as well as all the other letters!

- Read aloud a list of words beginning with the phoneme /n/ and ask the children to knock on the floor or call out 'knock, knock' if it's a word with a silent 'k'.
- Ask the children to write a list of the words beginning with /n/ and use a fluorescent pen to highlight the silent 'k' when they write one.

Variation

- The children could stick a door that opens onto a piece of coloured card. They could write 'knock knock' on the door and write 'silent k' on the back of the door, then write a list of 'silent k' words inside.

Cross-curricular link

English: extending vocabulary knowledge.

The Very Hungry Caterpillar

Use the ideas in this popular book to encourage children to read and write the days of the week.

Suitable for

Children who are learning graphemes of more than one letter.

Aims

To encourage children to read and write the days of the week.

Resources

- Carle, E. (2002) *The Very Hungry Caterpillar*, London: Hamish Hamilton
- Seven pieces of card with the start of the sentences printed for each day of the week, e.g. *On Monday he ate ...*
- Seven identical blank strips of card for the ending of the sentences

What to do

- Read and enjoy the book together.
- Working with a small group, tell the children they are going to help you write a new story about the caterpillar.
- Show the children the first card and read it together, segmenting the word *Monday*.
- Ask the children for ideas about what different food he might eat and write this on a matching strip of card for the end of the sentence, e.g. *an egg*.
- Continue with the rest of the days of the week, encouraging the children, and include Saturday when he eats a list of treats and then has tummy ache.

- Explain to the children that many of the names of the days are tricky words, but encourage them to notice that all the days end with *d-ay* and try to identify some other known phonemes in each of the names of the days, e.g. *S -a -t* at the beginning of Saturday.
- Finally, encourage the children to choose a healthy vegetable for Sunday and help them to segment the name of the day.
- Now distribute the broken sentences to a group of children, giving one day of the week to each child and asking them to find the correct ending for their sentence.
- The children can copy out the complete sentences ready for you to stick them into a class book.
  Perhaps some other children could illustrate the sentences for the new story.
- When the book is finished, leave it available for the children to read.

Variation

- More able children could use the start of the sentences and picture dictionaries to write their own stories into little books or on a suitable computer program.

Cross-curricular link

PSHE: healthy eating.

The Lighthouse Keeper's Lunch

 Play a memory game to build compound words.

Suitable for

Children who are learning graphemes of more than one letter.

Aims

To read short words that use familiar graphemes, and then use them to make longer words.

Resources

- Armitage, R. (2007) *The Lighthouse Keeper's Lunch*, London: Scholastic
- Word cards:

   sea (x3), side, shore, weed
   ice (x2), lolly, cream
   sand (x2), wich, castle, dune
   swim, suit
   wind, break
   sail, boat
   tide, line
   pic, nic

What to do

- Read and enjoy the story of Mr Grinling in his lighthouse.
- Discuss some of the features of the seaside that can be seen in the book.
  Talk about any other seaside experiences that the children may have had.
  Identify some of the main features that you will be using for the game.

- Have the cards ready in pairs. Take one pair and show them to the children. Help them to read each word on its own, and then demonstrate how they can be put together to make a new word.
- Go through all of the cards, encouraging the children to read them.
- Sit a small group of children round a table with the word cards spread out face-down on the table.
- The first child turns two cards over, leaving them in their place, and reads them out loud. Can they be put together to make a new word? If so, the child picks them up and keeps them. If not, they are turned over in their place.
- The next child turns two cards over. If he reads the first one as he turns it over he might realise that one of the original cards will make a pair with it. Can he remember where it was?
- Continue until all of the cards have been successfully paired. The winner is the one with the most pairs. Give them a clap!
- Children could record their pairs – by writing and drawing.

Variation

- The words could be added to your word bank if you are currently working on a seaside theme, or used as labels on a display.

Cross·curricular link

Geography: places.

Huff and puff

Use the wolf's dialogue to encourage children to make new words by changing the initial letter of words.

Suitable for

Children who are learning graphemes of more than one letter.

Aims

To help children practise oral blending skills.

What to do

- Retell the story of the three little pigs together, encouraging the children to join in with the wolf's dialogue:
  I'll huff and I'll puff and I'll blow your house down.
- Write the words *huff* and *puff* on the board.
- Ask the children what difference they can see between the two words.
- Write up a few other words that can change the initial sound to /p/:
  hen, hill, hat, hot, hump, hole, hay, hit, hop, hatch, hark, hale, hack, had, hip, holly, hope, hull, hunt.
- Sit in a circle and let the first child say a word beginning with /h/ and then pick another child in the circle to change the initial sound of that word to a /p/ and make a new word.
- If you don't want to record the words, you might think it appropriate to accept rhyming words that have alternative spellings, such as *hair/pear, high/pie, hour/power, hurl/pearl*. Or challenge the more able children to spell these words correctly.

Variation

- Give the children a list of six words beginning with /h/ and ask them to write new words by changing the initial letter to /p/.

Cross-curricular link

English: being aware of rhyming words.

This is the Bear and the Picnic Lunch

A circle game using rhyming words, focusing on a range of different initial phonemes.

Suitable for

Children who are practising single-letter sounds and graphemes of more than one letter.

Aims

To help children use and identify a range of phonemes.

Resources

- Hayes, S. (2003) *This is the Bear and the Picnic Lunch*, London: Walker Books Ltd

---

What to do

- Read and enjoy the book.
- Sit in a circle and teach the children this rhyme:

    Munch crunch
    Munch crunch
    What did ... (someone) ... eat for lunch?

- Explain to the children that they are going to complete the final sentence with a name. It should be the name of someone in the class.
- Start the game off with everyone repeating the rhyme together, then you say one child's name in the last line. This child tells everyone a food they like to eat. Then the class recites the poem and the named child chooses another child to name in the last line and the game continues.

- Once the children have got the idea, stop the game and tell them you're going to make it a bit harder now. Explain that the food they suggest this time must start with the same sound as their name, e.g.

  Munch crunch
  Munch crunch
  What did Lily eat for lunch?

  Lily might say *liquorice* or *lamb chops* or *lollipops*.
  Then all say:

  Munch crunch
  Munch crunch
  What did ... (Lily names another child from the class) *eat for lunch?*

- Continue playing until everyone's had a turn. If any child struggles to think of a food, either you can make a suggestion or you can ask the other children for ideas. The child whose turn it is can then choose which food they want to say and the game continues.

Variation

- You can play this game with the children taking turns to choose animals instead of children's names:

  Munch crunch
  Munch crunch
  What did ... rhino eat for lunch?

  They might say *rice* or *risotto* or *red cabbage*.

Cross-curricular link

DT: food.

Nothing

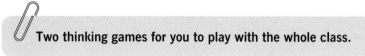

Two thinking games for you to play with the whole class.

Suitable for

Children who are learning graphemes of more than one letter.

Aims

To provide children with an opportunity to use and read the phoneme /th/.

Resources

- Inkpen, M. (2006) *Nothing*, London: Hodder Children's Books

What to do

- Write the word *nothing* on the board and read the word together.
- Can the children work out how many phonemes make up the word? After a few children have made suggestions, identify the five phonemes: /n/ o/ th/ i/ ng.
- Focus on the middle phoneme. Can anyone suggest a word that begins with this sound?
- Listen to the children's suggestions – be aware that there may be some confusion with the phoneme /f/. Demonstrate the different position of the tongue to produce the /th/ sound.
  E.g. 'think' begins with this sound.
- Tell the children you are going to play a game and everyone has to think of something beginning with /th/.
- Sit in a circle and start the game off by saying 'I'm thinking of ... 'thunder', then ask the child next to you, 'What are you thinking of?' This child repeats, 'I'm thinking of ... (and suggests something beginning with /th/).

- Explain to the children that if they can't think of anything then they can use the word on the board and say 'I'm thinking of nothing!'

  Ideas could include: *theatre*, *thermometer*, *three*, *thirteen*, *thick*, *things*, *thank you*, *thirsty*, *throat*, *thin*.

Variation

- Try thinking of three things. Divide the children into groups of three. Each group must think of three things on a theme beginning with the phoneme /th/. Themes could be:

  Three thin things
  Three thick things
  Three things you can thread
  Three things to be thankful for
  Three things to do on Thursday
  Three things you can throw

  Have the themes written out on pieces of card. Hold up the card and read it together. Allow a short time for them to discuss ideas in their groups. Then each group lists their best three ideas. The group with the most ingenious three ideas are the winners. Play the game again with a different theme. NOTE: Their ideas do not have to begin with the phoneme.

Cross-curricular link

PSHE: playing cooperatively.

Chapter 3
Stage C

Where the Wild Things Are

Use this super book to inspire children to play with language and learn to spell some tricky words.

Suitable for

Children who are learning alternative graphemes.

Aims

To help children read and spell words tricky words – *here*, *there*, *where*.

Resources

- Sendak, M. (1992) *Where the Wild Things Are*, London: Picture Lions, imprint of HarperCollins

What to do

- Read and enjoy the book together.
- Look at the title. Explain that the author will have thought very carefully about his title. Write the words on separate pieces of card.
- Change the position of the word 'are' and ask the children what they notice about the new sentence.
  Where are *the wild things?*
  Read the question with the appropriate intonation.
  Remind the children that if they were writing this they would need a question mark.
- Can the words be moved again to create a different question?
  The wild things are where?
  Maybe some in the class would like to read the question with mock horror!

Remind the children that if they were writing this question it would need a question mark and a capital letter.

- Tell the children that all three sentences are concerned with the placement of words.
- Write the words *where*, *there* and *here* on the board.
  Tell the children that all these words are concerned with place.
  Do the children notice they share the same spelling pattern?
- Ask the children to create some sentences about the wild things by changing *where* for *there* and *here*, e.g.

    Here are the wild things.
    The wild things are there.

- The children might like to redesign the cover of the book with their new titles.

Variation

- More able children might enjoy creating some compound words with the base word 'where'. E.g. *somewhere* or *nowhere* or *everywhere* or *anywhere*. They could try out different options using these words to replace 'where' in the title and then choose the new title they like the best. E.g. *Are the wild things anywhere?*

Cross-curricular link

English: wordplay.

Don't Forget the Bacon

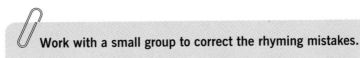

Work with a small group to correct the rhyming mistakes.

Suitable for

Children who are learning alternative graphemes.

Aims

To encourage children to hear rhymes and explore a range of alternative graphemes.

Resources

*   Hutchins, P. (1978) *Don't Forget the Bacon*, London: Picture Puffins

What to do

*   After enjoying the story with a small group, discuss what happens in the story – why does the boy get the shopping list all mixed up?
*   Tell them you want them to find the rhyming mistakes.
    Can anyone remember an example from the story?
*   Write up the four items in the original list that the boy has to buy. Taking each one in turn, decide what they are changed into.
    E.g. *Six farm eggs – six fat legs – six clothes pegs*.
*   Write the phrases on the board and encourage the children to read them aloud. Clap the rhythm of the three words.
*   Can the children spot the rhyming words in each phrase:
    legs, pegs, eggs.
*   Ask the children to work out the other changes to the second item on the shopping list:
    A cake for tea – a cape for me – a rake for leaves.
    Can they spot what happens to the rhymes here? Sometimes writers use near-rhymes.

- *A pound of pears – a flight of stairs – a pile of chairs.*
  Do the children notice the different spelling pattern here?
- Finally, what happened to the bacon?

Variation

- You may be able to write a new shopping list together that becomes altered:

  bananas could become *pyjamas*
  ice cream could become *a bad dream*
  plums could become *drums*
  mushrooms could become *bedrooms*
  cheese could become *bees* or *knees*
  an ice lolly could become *a new dolly*

  Have fun!

Cross-curricular link

English: rhyming words.

'The Chocolate Soldier'

Use this amusing poem to highlight two ways to spell the phoneme /e/.

Suitable for

Children who are learning alternative graphemes.

Aims

To focus children's attention on two different spellings of phoneme /e/.

Resources

- Foster, J. (chosen by) (2003) *Completely Crazy Poems*, London: Collins, imprint of HarperCollins

What to do

- Read the poem 'The Chocolate Soldier' by Granville Lawson.
- When they have enjoyed the rhyme a few times and the laughter subsides, ask the children to identify the two rhyming words.
- Write out the poem as the children recite it, missing out the two rhyming words.
- Segment the word 'red' and choose someone to write it and complete line two.
- Segment the word 'spread' but explain that it is written differently. Does anyone know how it might be spelt?
- Ask a child to write 'spread' to complete line four of the poem. Does anyone know another word that is spelt a similar way? E.g. 'head'.
- Tell the children they are going to use this poem as a framework for their own poem.

- Ask for ideas of something different that might be crossing the road instead of the soldier.
  Ideas that fit the rhythm of the poem might include a chocolate: *fairy, hedgehog, teddy, rabbit, giant*.
  Other ideas: *pussy cat, Easter egg, Humpty Dumpty, dinosaur, tortoise, elephant, frog, doll*.
- Encourage the children to substitute their new character into the poem in place of the soldier.
- Let the children write out their new poems and decorate them.

Variation

- You could also segment the word 'said', since it rhymes with red, and use this opportunity to draw their attention to the spelling of /e/ in this tricky word.

Cross-curricular link

English: poetry.

The Copper Tin Cup

Make up some names for mystery family members.

Suitable for

Children who are learning alternative graphemes.

Aims

To recreate a story with the children, choosing names with the same initials.

Resources

- Schaefer, C.L. (2000) *The Copper Tin Cup*, London: Walker
- An old metal cup, if possible
- Photocopies of the sentences for children to copy (see below)

What to do

- Share this book with the children. It tells the story of how Sammy Carl came to own this cup that has his initials on it. They are the same initials as his mother, his grandfather and his great aunt – and the cup originally belonged to her.
- Ask the children if they know their own initials. If they have two first names, use them. The children may want to invent a second name for themselves if they don't actually have one.
- Show them the metal cup and ask them to imagine that it has their initials on it. Ask a few children to tell you what their cup would have on it.
- Remind the children that the cup in the story belonged to different people in the past. Now they should imagine that this cup belonged to someone else in their family before them. Can they invent a name for this person so that it uses the same initials as they have? Again ask for examples, e.g., *My name is Ben Andrew. My daddy had this cup before me. He is called Billy Alan.*

My name is Sarah Jane. My mummy had this cup before me. Her name is Susan Jean.

- In these examples the initial letter is pronounced as it is written. Be aware that children may suggest names where the grapheme is part of an alternative phoneme, e.g. Cecilia sounds like Sarah but won't have the same initial. They have to match the grapheme for this activity to make sense.
- Give the children a copy of the sentences with key words missing. It should say:

    My name is ...
    My ... had this cup before me.
    Their name is ...

- They can now complete the sentences and draw a picture to show each person with the cup. Some children may be able to go back one more generation and identify 'their' grandparent.

Variation

- Children can create their initials on a paper cup by gluing string on in the shape of the letters. When it's dry they can wrap kitchen foil round the paper cup, and gently press and mould the string initials so that they show through.

Cross-curricular link

History: people in the past.

Chocolate Mousse for Greedy Goose

A fabulous book to stimulate children's interest in rhyming words.

Suitable for

Children who are learning alternative graphemes.

Aims

To stimulate children's interest in rhyming words and their spellings.

Resources

- Donaldson, J. (2005) *Chocolate Mousse for Greedy Goose*, London: Macmillan Children's Books

What to do

- Read and enjoy the book together.
- Read it again, pausing before the rhyming word for the children to provide the word.
- Write out the rhyming pairs.
  Segment the words to identify the rhyming phonemes and discuss with the children how some words share the same spelling of the rhyming phoneme while others use an alternative.
- Ask the children to make two lists, one of words that share the same spelling pattern and the other for words that use different ones e.g. *yuck – duck/you – kangaroo.*
- Can the children think of rhymes for other animals on the theme of eating?
  Ideas might include:
    I've come for tea – said Bumble Bee
    Just lick it – said Cricket

Eat a juicy pear – said Bear
Shiny fish – has a large dish
More for me – said Little Flea
Butterfly – wants apple pie

- Write them out for the children to read. They might enjoy illustrating their new rhymes in the style of Nick Sharratt's wonderful illustrations.

Variation

- When you've discussed the rhymes and thought up some new ones, try playing a circle game. A child names an animal and a child opposite them across the circle responds with a rhyming word or phrase.

Cross-curricular link

English: responding to literature.

Iris and Isaac

A touching story exploring friendship that provides a stimulus for spotting various spellings of the phoneme /igh/.

Suitable for

Children who are learning alternative graphemes.

Aims

To help children develop an understanding of the spellings of the phoneme /igh/.

Resources

- Rayner, C. (2010) *Iris and Isaac*, London: Little Tiger Press, an imprint of Magi Publications

What to do

- Read and enjoy the book together.
- Discuss the theme of friendship and sharing.
- Look at the names in the title. Who can spot what's the same in each name?
- Draw the children's attention to the capital 'I' at the beginning of both names. Both names begin with the same letter, pronounced as /igh/ in these names.
  Remind the children that we write the word **I** with this capital letter. Can they think of any other words that begin with the /igh/ phoneme? E.g. *idea*.
- Ask the children to listen out for this phoneme /igh/ as you reread the story.
  Perhaps they can raise their hand every time they hear the /igh/ phoneme.

E.g. When the friends separate:

    Iris sees a flock of eiders high in the sky

    Isaac spots two foxes playing on the ice

    and the Northern lights.

- Identify the grapheme for /igh/ in each of the words.
- Draw five columns on the board and write *Iris* in the first, *eider* in the second, *high* in the third, *sky* in the fourth and *ice* in the fifth.
- Challenge the children to find another word that follows these spelling patterns. E.g.

    Iris/island/I/ivy/find

    eider/either/neither

    high/light/sigh/night/fight

    sky/my/why/fry

    ice/spice/nice/rice – like/time/slide/ripe

- Which column has the most? Which has the least?
- Can they suggest any other ways of spelling the /igh/ phoneme? E.g. *pie*, *eye*.

Variation

- Use the children's suggestions of words containing the /igh/ phoneme to write different experiences for the friends, e.g.

    Iris saw a long slippery slide

    Isaac found a ripe juicy pear.

Cross-curricular link

PSHE: developing good relationships.

The Usborne Book of Dinosaurs

Use children's fascination with dinosaurs to help them learn to spell their names.

Suitable for

Children who are learning alternative graphemes.

Aims

To provide a stimulus for children to practise alternative graphemes of the phoneme /or/.

Resources

- Mayes, S. (2004) *The Usborne Book of Dinosaurs*, London: Usborne Publishing

What to do

- Discuss the children's favourite dinosaurs.
- Focus the children's attention on dinosaur names.
- Notice how many of them end with the suffix – *saurus*.
  Explain that this is the Greek word for lizard or reptile.
- Write the word 'dinosaur' on the board and ask the children to segment the word d-i-n-o-s-aur.
- Ask who can spot how the /or/ sound is spelt in dinosaur.
- Then write up one of the many dinosaur names that have this spelling. E.g. *Brontosaurus*, *Apatosaurus*, *Tyrannosaurus*, *Albertosaurus*, *Bactrosaurus*.
- Tell the children you want them to write 'I saw a dinosaur'.
  Who knows how to write 'I saw...'?
  The children may have already been taught this as a tricky word but this is an opportunity to use the word to illustrate another spelling of the /or/ phoneme.

- When you have confirmed that these are two different spellings of the phoneme /or/, let the children write the sentence with dinosaurs of their choice:
  I saw a ... Brontosaurus.
  Remind everyone to start their dinosaur sentence with a capital and end with a full stop.
- When the children have written several sentences they can illustrate their work with drawings of some of the named dinosaurs.

Variation

- When the children have finished their writing you could sit together and let them take turns to ask who saw one of the dinosaurs on their list. Count up the answers – which dinosaur was chosen by the most people?

Cross-curricular link

History: prehistoric life.

'Row, row, row your boat'

Have a go at doing the actions for this before making a moveable figure.

Suitable for

Children who are practising alternative graphemes.

Aims

To encourage children to remember the alternative graphemes 'oa' and 'ow' for the phoneme /oa/.

Resources

- Each child needs a combined head and body piece – in profile, two arms and two legs, and two split pins

What to do

- Sing the rhyme together to make sure everyone knows the words.
- Find a partner and sit facing each other, hold hands and then move forwards and backwards in time with the rhythm of your singing.
- Write the title of this song on the whiteboard. Ask one of the children to point to the words as everyone reads them out.

- Ask a child to come out and put a line under the letters in 'row' that make the /oa/ sound – 'ow'. Some children may benefit from repeating this with each of the three 'row' words. Then ask a child to underline the /oa/ sound in 'boat'. What do they notice? Does anyone spot that the same sound is written in two different ways?
- You could make up silly first lines for the rhyme, following the spelling patterns of the original, e.g.

   Throw, throw, throw your coat
   Show, show, show your goat

- Now make some figures.
  Use one split pin to go through both arms and the body – one arm in front and one behind. Do the same with the legs.
- The figure can now be moved. Children can work with their partner to arrange their figures facing each other on a sheet of paper or card to look as if they are doing the actions to the rhyme. Fix them securely in place. Children may want to add hair, features and to colour in some 'clothes'.

Variation

- You can use the finished pairs of figures to create a display with water and boats. Give it the heading: *Row, row, row your boat*.

Cross-curricular link

DT: assembling and joining components.

100 Things You Should Know About Polar Lands

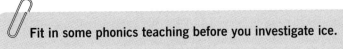

Fit in some phonics teaching before you investigate ice.

Suitable for

Children who are practising alternative graphemes.

Aims

To show the children a different way to write the phoneme /z/, using 'ze'.

Resources

- Parker, S. (2008) *100 Things You Should Know About Polar Lands*, Gt Bardfield, Essex: Miles Kelly Publishing
  Write up the story:

  > *There's a strong breeze blowing at the North Pole.*
  > *A very cold strong breeze.*
  > *Polar Bear takes shelter in his ice-cave.*
  > *He starts to sneeze. He starts to wheeze.*
  > *Poor Polar Bear! If only he could get warm ...*
  > *How can we help him? What can we try?*

- For the science: ice cubes, plastic cups with lids and warm water, pieces of blanket, a hot water bottle, etc.

What to do

- Ask the children to segment the word 'tree'. Write it down as they tell you the sounds: /t/ /r/ /ee/.
- Now ask them to sound out the word 'trees', and write it down underneath 'tree'. Which letter makes the sound /z/? The 's'.

- Now ask the children to segment 'free', and write it. Then 'frees' and write it. What does this mean? Can they put it into a sentence? E.g., *The fisherman frees the line that has got caught.*
- Explain to the children that in your work on ice you will need to use the word 'freeze'. This rhymes with 'trees', and sounds the same as 'frees' but doesn't have the same spelling pattern. This time it is spelt 'f-r-e-e-z-e'.
- Write the word 'freeze' on the board underneath the word 'frees'. Look for similarities. Then spot the /z/ sound. Which letters make that sound? 'ze'.
- Ask the children if they know any other words that rhyme with 'freeze'. They shouldn't be plurals as there are lots of them! They might suggest: *cheese, ease, please, breeze, sneeze, wheeze.*
- Set the scene for their science work by showing them Polar Bear's problem, which you have written out. Read it together. Notice the 'ze' words.
- Children can now do the science investigation based on Polar Bear's problem.

Variation

- Make up your own story of Polar Bear, his cold and the solutions he tries. Use as many words that end with /z/ as you can.

Cross-curricular link

Science: freezing and melting.

Mister Magnolia

Enjoy this wittily rhyming book and learn different spellings for the phoneme /oo/.

Suitable for

Children who are learning alternative phonemes.

Aims

To help children learn alternative spellings for the phoneme /oo/.

Resources

- Blake, Q. (2010) *Mister Magnolia*, London: Red Fox, Random House Children's Books

What to do

- Enjoy the book together, noticing the rhymes.
- Ask the children what we know about Mister Magnolia from reading the book.
  What possessions does he have? What are his hobbies? Who are his family? What pets does he have? How does he have fun?
- List all the information about Mister Magnolia on the board.
- Write *boot* at the top of the list and when you are ready to write *suit* remind the children that it rhymes with *boot* but ask them to watch carefully as you write the word. *What do you notice?*
- Explain to the children that in this word the /oo/ phoneme is created by the 'ui'.
- Now ask the children to help you write the rhyming phrase for each item listed, e.g. *Two fat owls ... learning to hoot.*

- How many different ways for spelling the /oo/ phoneme can the children spot?

    'oo' in *boot, toot, hoot, scoot*

    'u-e' in *flute, chute, brute, salute*

    'ui' in *suit, fruit*

    'ew' in *newt, new*

- If you want to include 'ue', ask the children what colour is Mister Magnolia's new boot!
- Help the children make a collage picture of Mister Magnolia with pictures of all his interests around him.
- Let the children make labels for each, using the rhyming words from the text.

Variation

- Collect together all the rhyming words. Ask the children to make lists, one for each of the different ways to write the /oo/ phoneme. Don't forget to include 'ue' by asking the children what colour is Mister Magnolia's new boot! Then challenge them to find other words to add to the lists. Which spelling is the most common for the phoneme /oo/?

Cross-curricular link

English: patterns of rhythm and rhyme.

Be Gentle

This lovely book encourages children to be gentle and illustrates an alternative grapheme for the phoneme /j/.

Suitable for

Children who are learning alternative graphemes.

Aims

To practise words that include the phoneme /j/ when spelt with a 'g'.

Resources

- Miller, V. (2001) *Be Gentle*, London: Walker Books Ltd

What to do

- Read and enjoy the book together. Discuss times when they need to be gentle.
- Look at the title of the book again. Point to each word in turn, focusing on the initial sound. Ask if anyone notices something strange about the word *'gentle'*.
- Remind the children that the phoneme /j/ can be written with a letter 'g'.
- Collect together all the words you can think of that begin with this grapheme: *general, gentleman, giant, ginger, gym, gem*.
- Then think of words that have this grapheme for the /j/ within words: *angel, magic, rigid, original, energy*.
- Finally, list the words that end with the grapheme 'ge' or 'dge': *age, wage, page, stage, strange, orange, edge, hedge, bridge, sledge, fudge*.
- Now play a guessing game with the words listed. Give clues to the word and the children have to guess which word it is, e.g. Clue: *People in the Christmas play danced on this*. Answer: *stage*.

- When the children have guessed a few words, ask if anyone would like to give a clue to one of the words. Then you can join in with the guessing!

Variation

- The game can be adapted to be played with groups of words that share the same spelling pattern.

Cross-curricular link

English: speaking and listening.

Mog's Amazing Birthday Caper

Enjoy this alliterative alphabet book and spot some alternative graphemes.

Suitable for

Children who are learning alternative graphemes.

Aims

To encourage children to appreciate alliteration and notice alternative graphemes.

Resources

- Kerr, J. (2002) *Mog's Amazing Birthday Caper*, London: Collins Picture Books

What to do

- Enjoy the book together, noticing the alliteration on each letter.
- Take time to explore some of the more complicated vocabulary too, e.g. *survivors*, *treacherous*, *vivid*.
- Remind the children that the same grapheme can be pronounced in different ways, then look through the book for examples, e.g.
  giraffe and *garden*
  ice cream and *Indian*
  outwitted and *overpowered*
- Write the grapheme and words from the book on the board, e.g. 'g' *garden* and *giraffe*.
- Ask the children if they can think of other examples, e.g. *great* and *giant*.
- Repeat with the other initials that demonstrate two sounds from one grapheme.

- Ask the children to work in pairs to write their own alliterative sentence for these initial letters.
- Display these under the heading *'One letter but two different sounds'*.

Variation

- Ask more able children to write a sentence with 'n' or 'r' and include some words that begin with a silent letter.

Cross-curricular link

English: learning the alphabet.

Chapter 4
Stage D

The Enormous Crocodile

> Use the opening sentence of this fabulous book to explore suffixes.

Suitable for

Children who are gaining confidence with spelling.

Aims

To help children use their knowledge of different spelling rules when adding the suffix 'est' to a word.

Resources

- Dahl, R. (2008) *The Enormous Crocodile*, London: Puffin Books

What to do

- Enjoy the story together.
- Tell the children you are going to look at the choices of words Roald Dahl has made.
- Read the opening sentence then write on the board: 'In a big brown muddy river'.
  Ask the children how this is different from what is written in the book.
- Look at the spelling of each word to see how it has changed by adding the suffix:
  big – double the final letter before adding 'est'.
  brown – no change, simply add 'est'.
  muddy – change the 'y' to 'i' before adding 'est'.
- Collect together other words that could describe a river, e.g. *deep, wide, thin, dirty, blue, clear, shallow, wet, cloudy*.

- Ask the children to choose three new words from the list and then tell you the new opening sentence they have created to describe the river. Remember to add the suffix 'est' to each new word as they say it.
- The teacher then scribes each new sentence asking for the children's input about the changes needed when adding the suffix. Point out to the children that words ending with the letter 'e' only need 'st' adding to complete the suffix.

Variation

- It might be appropriate to let the children work in pairs to create their new sentences and then write their new sentences themselves.

Cross-curricular link

English: author study on Roald Dahl.

About Your Body

> **Learn about the body, then focus on spelling as you make labels for each part.**

Suitable for

Children who are gaining confidence with spelling.

Aims

To provide a context for children to use their knowledge of alternative graphemes.

Resources

- Taylor, B. (2001) *Everyday Science: About Your Body*, London: Hodder Children's Books
- Outline of a body for each child

What to do

- Read the book together and discuss different body parts.
- Give each child an outline of a body.
- Everyone can take a turn naming one part of the body and the other children point to the position of the part on their outline.
- Explain to the children that they are to label the parts of the body. Ask the children to segment the first label, e.g. *head*.
- Write 'h' on the board then ask how the /e/ phoneme is written in the word *head*. Does anyone know how to spell the word? Can anyone make a suggestion?
- Repeat the process with each body part. Some are simple, e.g. *leg*. Others offer practise with graphemes of more than one letter, e.g. *arm*.
  Labels that offer practise with alternative graphemes include: h**ea**d, f**oo**t, elb**ow**, ne**ck**, **ea**r, **eye**, ank**le**.
  Knee and *wrist* also provide examples of silent letters.

- It may be appropriate to encourage some children to now write the labels independently, while others may need to copy the labels.

Variation

- Print the words on card labels that can be cut up into phonemes. Then let small groups of children decide which phoneme fits in each word as they rebuild the labels.

Cross-curricular link

Science: the human body.

Starting to Measure

Introduce the phoneme /zh/ as you have fun with measuring.

Suitable for

Children who are gaining confidence with spelling.

Aims

To help children remember that the letter 's' is sometimes pronounced as a hard /zh/ sound.

Resources

- Bryant-Mole, K. (1999) *Starting to Measure*, London: Usborne First Learning
- Rulers, tape measures
- Card, squared paper

What to do

- The word 'measure' contains the /zh/ phoneme. Show the word to the children as you introduce a measuring activity. Encourage them to say the word and feel the vibration of the sound /zh/ on their tongue.
- These activities focus on the words: *measure, measurements, treasure, leisure, television*.
  Draw the children's attention to these words as you use them.
- If you want to know how big your television is you have to *measure* the diagonal of the screen. Try finding some diagonal *measurements*.
  Measure one side of a box across the diagonal.
  Measure and cut out a piece of paper based on this diagonal *measurement*.

Draw a picture on it and stick it on the front of the box to make a *television* screen.

Use it in your role-play area.

- If you are a pirate, try making a map to show where you have buried your *treasure*.

    You may write out the instructions, such as, start at the palm tree and take five steps north, then 10 steps east, then *measure* the length of two spades before starting to dig.

    Make a net of a box using specific *measurements*. Fold it and stick the sides together to make a *treasure* chest. Decorate it and display with your pirate maps.

- Draw a plan of a *leisure* centre. On your plan the *measurements* are: the whole building = 20cm x 30cm, the pool = 15cm x 10cm, the changing rooms = 5cm x 5cm, etc.

- Make labels for your displays, or instructions for the activities, so that children have a chance to practise reading the words with the /zh/ phoneme.

Variation

- Children who are ready to discover that the two colour words 'beige' and 'azure' contain this phoneme could create patterns using the /zh/ colours. Both words originate from Old French words.

Cross-curricular link

Maths: measuring.

Number rhyme

> Use a familiar number rhyme to encourage children to write their own version and explore a range of alternative graphemes.

Suitable for

Children who are gaining confidence with spelling.

Aims

To encourage children to explore a range of alternative graphemes.

Resources

- A copy of a traditional rhyme that uses numbers, e.g. 'Oliver Twist' in Waters, F. (1999) *Time for a Rhyme*, London: Orion Children's Books

What to do

- Enjoy the traditional number rhyme together.
- Ask the children to list the numbers one to ten down the left side of a piece of paper in this form:
  Number one
  Number two
  Number three
  Number four, etc.
  (Decide if it's appropriate to use numbers 1–5 or 1–10.)
- When they have done this, repeat the rhyme and identify the rhyming word for each number, e.g.
  one – tongue
  two – shoe
  three – knee
  four – floor
  five – alive

six – sticks
seven – heaven
eight – gate
nine – line
ten – again

- Compare the spellings of the numbers to their rhyming word.
- Can the children suggest alternatives and invent a new rhyme?
- Write out suggested alternative rhyming words against the numbers on the board, e.g.

    one – swan or *gone*
    two – stew or *Boo!*
    three – tree or *flea*
    four – door or *snore*
    five – dive or *hive*
    six – tricks or *mix*
    seven – eleven or *Devon*
    eight – wait or *plate*
    nine – spine or *sign*
    ten – hen or *when*

- Ask the children to make up a new rhyming phrase using one of these words with each of the numbers.
    (It may be appropriate for the children to work in pairs.)
- Read the new rhymes out loud.

Variation

- Work together during a shared writing session to write one class rhyme.

Cross-curricular link

Mathematics: writing number words.

Mirror, mirror on the wall

Use the idea of the magic mirror from Snow White to encourage children to add the suffix 'est' to a range of words.

Suitable for

Children who are gaining confidence with spelling.

Aims

To encourage children to add the suffix 'est' to a range of root words.

Resources

- A mirror or sheet of smooth foil (or let the children make a cardboard frame decorated with pasta shapes and sprayed gold)
- A large piece of card to display below the mirror with the words:

  Mirror, mirror on the wall
  who is the ... of them all?

- A box containing a selection of root words printed on cards: *fair, sweet, kind, old, young, tall, small, fast, clever, neat, smart*; make these cards long enough to add the suffix 'est' on the end
- A copy of the traditional fairy story *Snow White*

What to do

- Discuss the story and the way the wicked stepmother uses the magic mirror.
- Show the children the mirror.
- Can the children remember what the wicked stepmother asks the mirror in the story?
- Read the printed question together and ask which word is missing.
- Show the children the card with the word *fair* and ask what has been added to this word to change it into the word *fairest*.

- Choose a child to write *est* onto the end of the word, then stick the word in place on the printed question.
- Reread the question and ensure the children understand the meaning of the word.
- Explain that you want to ask the magic mirror a different question and choose a child to select a new word from the box.
- Read the new word together and ask how it needs changing to fit into the question.
- Select a different child to write the suffix on this word and put the new word in the question and read it together, e.g.,

    Mirror, mirror on the wall
    *Who is the **kindest** of them all?*

- Discuss with the children what the mirror would answer today. Who do they think has been very kind recently? Choose someone in the class and give them a round of applause!
- Continue in the same way with the remaining root words.

Variation

- If you play the game again, perhaps you could include some words that need to change their ending before the suffix can be added. Explore these with the children and help them write the whole new word on the reverse of the card. Suggestions could be:

    funny, happy, busy, pretty – change 'y' to 'i' before adding suffix
    sad – double final consonant before adding suffix
    cute, brave – retain the final 'e' and just add 'st'.

Cross-curricular link

PSHE: respecting differences between people.

Toddle Waddle

Use this super rhyming book about sounds to create a dance performance.

Suitable for

Children who are gaining confidence with spelling.

Aims

To stimulate children's interest in rhyming words and spelling.

Resources

- Donaldson, J. (2009) *Toddle Waddle*, London: Macmillan Children's Books

What to do

- Enjoy the book together, identifying how the various sound effects are made.
- Ask the children what they notice about the two words *toddle* and *waddle* – perhaps they'll say they rhyme.
- Then ask them what similarities and differences they can see in the spellings.
  It might be appropriate to mention that when the /o/ phoneme follows the letter 'w' it's often written as a letter 'a', e.g. *was*.
  How many other words can the children think of?
  E.g. *wash, want, wander, watch*.
- As you go through the book, encourage the children to explore the other rhyming words in the story.
  Examples of questions to ask could include:
  – How many pairs of rhyming words change the vowel?
  – How is the /ee/ phoneme spelt in *leap* and *creep*?
  – How many change the initial consonant to create a rhyming word?
  – What grapheme makes the /s/ phoneme in *dance, prance*?

- Which sound effects are described by repeating a word? E.g. *choo choo*.
- Take the children into a large space and practise the actions and sound effects for the pairs of rhyming words.
- Choose a pair of children to repeat each of the rhymes as they act out the actions, e.g. one child leaps and the second child creeps.
- Perform the sound effects from the whole book:
  - Start with the eight characters on the walk.
  - Who then stop to survey the beach scene (introducing eleven more characters)?
  - Take the train ride (behind a train driver).
  - Enjoy the music at the band stand (five or more characters).
  - Finally everyone stops and waves and shouts bye-bye!

Variation

- Try creating a new story told through sound effects: you could change the order of the characters or events or invent some new ones, e.g. maybe a fire engine might go by?

Cross-curricular link

PE: create and perform dances.

Two Can, Toucan

Have fun with word play as you share your favourite jokes.

Suitable for

Children who are gaining confidence with spelling.

Aims

To help the children understand how they can use similar-sounding words to create jokes.

Resources

- McKee, D. (1969) *Two Can, Toucan*, Middlesex: Picture Puffin, Penguin Books Joke books, such as: Hill, H. (2010) *Harry Hill's Whopping Great Joke Book*, London: Faber and Faber Ltd

What to do

- Read the Mckee book together, and then look again at the title. Ask the children if they notice what the author has done to make this title. Do they spot the play on words?
- Explain to the children that this is how many jokes are created – by taking words that sound similar but mean different things, e.g. *Where would you find a book that isn't true? In the lie-brary (library)*.
- Write this up, so that the children can see the way that this works.
- Now write this one up:
  How would you surprise an Australian pudding? Boo! Meringue.
  Ask for a volunteer to read it out loud. Can anyone tell you what other word sounds like this? *Boomerang*. Write it on the board.

- Children may know some jokes that work in the same way, by playing on words. They could share them with the group, coming to the front one at a time. You will have to help them decide if it is word play or not.
- Give everyone a piece of A5 paper on which they can write out a joke. These can be fixed together as a class joke book.

Variation

- This could be a homework task as long as you write down some clear instructions for parents/carers about the need for the joke to be based on a word that has two meanings or two words that sound the same, e.g.

  mince pie/mince spy
  suck seed/succeed
  mobile phone/mobile foam

Cross-curricular link

English: word play.

'I had a little pet'

Use this amusing poem to stimulate interest in alternative graphemes.

Suitable for

Children who are gaining confidence with spelling.

Aims

To raise children's awareness of the different spellings of rhyming words.

Resources

- Foster, J. (chosen by) (2003) *Completely Crazy Poems*, London: Collins, imprint of HarperCollins

What to do

- Read the poem 'I had a little pet' by Colin Thompson.
- When the children have enjoyed the poem and illustration, ask which two words rhyme in this poem.
- Write the two words on the board – *worm* and *perm*.
- Help the children segment the words into their three phonemes, and encourage the children to tell you why the words rhyme and identify how the phoneme /ur/ is spelt in each word.
- Tell the children you'd like to write a new version of this poem with a different animal.
- Write the first line as the original, then in the second line replace the word *worm* with *horse*. Ask if anyone can think of a word that rhymes with horse.
  E.g. *sauce* or *of course*.

- Segment two new rhyming words and identify the alternative spellings of the phonemes shared in each word.
- Try fitting their suggestions into the poem's structure verbally before writing out the third line of the poem and creating a new last line, e.g. *I covered him in sauce* or *I made him pink of course*.
- Explore a few other ideas for new versions of this poem in the same way.

  Here are two other ideas that will provide opportunities for exploring alternative graphemes:

  fox and *socks*

  ghost and *toast*
- The children might enjoy illustrating one of the poems.

Variation

- Let the children write their own versions of the poem with their choice of pet and rhyming word, even if the words share the same spelling pattern, e.g.

  parrot and *carrot*

  pig and *wig*

  cat and *hat*

Cross-curricular link

English: poetry.

Floating and Sinking

An active game where children decide what rule applies when adding 'ing'.

Suitable for

Children who are gaining confidence with spelling.

Aims

To give children practise in adding 'ing' to a range of words.

Resources

- Riley, P. (2001) *Floating and Sinking (Ways into Science)*, London: Franklin Watts
- Labels printed in three distinct colours:
    double the final consonant before adding 'ing'
    take off the 'e' before adding 'ing'
    add 'ing'
- Verbs printed on individual cards:
    cut, sit, hop, tap, hum, run, put
    smile, slide, shake, use, wave, bike, dance
    float, sink, jump, fly, pull, walk, rock

What to do

- After enjoying the book together, look at the title of the book. Identify the ending that has been added to the base words *float* and *sink*.
- Ask what kind of words *float* and *sink* are.
  Can the children think of other verbs? Suggestions might include: *sing, burn, pull, fly, walk*.
- Challenge the children to add 'ing' to the verbs.

- Now ask the children to suggest a verb that ends with the letter 'e', e.g. *smile*.
  Remind the children to take off the 'e' before adding 'ing' to this type of word.
- Now ask the children to suggest a verb that has only one letter after the vowel, e.g. *cut*.
  Remind the children to double the final consonant before adding 'ing' to this type of word.
- Take the children into a large space and fix the three labels in different areas of the room where they are clearly visible to the children.
- Show the children the card that reads *walk* and ask the children to walk around the room until you clap your hands.
- Call out 'What are you doing?', and as the children answer *walking*, they must now decide what rule applies when adding 'ing' to this verb and run to the area displaying the label with the correct rule.
- Praise the children who work out the rule quickly and get to the area first.
- The children then return to the centre of the room and the game continues with you holding up a different verb.

Variation

- To play a quieter version, stick the labels on three tubs and put the cards into a pile. Let a small group of children take turns to pick up the cards and place them in the correct tub.

Cross-curricular link

Science: forces and motion.

The Paper Bag Princess

Use this unusual princess book to inspire the children to spell simple words.

Suitable for

Children who are gaining confidence with spelling.

Aims

To encourage children to spell simple words.

Resources

- Munsch, N. (1982) *The Paper Bag Princess*, London: Scholastic Publications
- Several paper bags
- Sets of eight cards with the individual letters *p, a, p, e, r, b, a, g* printed on each one

What to do

- Read and enjoy the book together. Discuss the story and characters.
- Look again at the title. Ask the children to segment the words 'paper bag' and 'princess'.
- Then identify and count the individual letters in 'paper bag'.
- Show the children one of the sets of these eight letters and stick them on a board.
- Demonstrate how to use the letters to spell simple words, e.g. *rag, gap, bap, beg, bear, pear, gear, ape, age, barge, rage, page*.
- Divide the children into pairs and give each pair a paper bag containing the eight letters.
- Ask them to make as many words as they can from the eight letters and record them in a list.
- When the children have spelt as many as they can, come back together and compare the lists.

Variation

- More able children could be set the challenge of using the word 'princess' (with or without providing individual letter cards) to see how many words they could spell, e.g. *in, is, ice, nice, rice, pin, pine, since, prince, rinse, price, spice, spine, sip, nip, rip, press*.

Cross-curricular link

English: wordplay.

If Pigs Could Fly ... and Other Deep Thoughts

Enjoy some poems and think about reading the grapheme 'ough'.

Suitable for

Children who are gaining confidence with spelling.

Aims

To provide an opportunity for children to practise reading the various pronunciations of the grapheme 'ough'.

Resources

- Lansky, B. (2006) *If Pigs Could Fly ... and Other Deep Thoughts*, Minnetonka, MN: Meadowbrook Press
- Cards with the following words on them – one word per card: *cough, rough, tough, through, although, drought, thorough, thought, ought, bought*

What to do

- Read and enjoy some of the poems from the book and then look again at the title.
- Now sound out the word 'thought' – /th/ /or/ /t/ and ask the children to tell you how many sounds there are in it. '3'.
- Tell the children that you want to write the word 'thought' on the whiteboard. Ask them to tell you how it is spelt by looking at the book title and calling out the letters to you as you write.
- Sound out the word again. Can anyone underline each of the three sounds as you say it? th – ough – t.
  Ask the children what sound the 'ough' makes? /or/.

- Ask the children if anyone can come out and write the word 'bought'. Tell them that it rhymes with 'thought', as well as having the same spelling pattern.
- Now try writing 'ought'.
- Choose one of the other 'ough' words from your cards and hold it up, e.g. *rough*. Who can read it? Children may read the 'ough' as /or/ or they may recognise the whole word.
  Point out the letters 'ough' and work out the sound they make. Is this the same as 'thought'?
- Go through the different cards reading, checking and working out the various sounds that this group of letters make:
  /o/ /f/ – cough
  /u/ /f/ – rough, tough
  /oo/ – through
  /oa/ – although
  /ow/ – drought
  ə – thorough

Variation

- Children can create some silly sentences with different 'ough' sounds in them. Ask your friend to read it out quickly. Can you make your friend's tongue get in a twist?
  E.g.

  He thought he had a rough cough.
  She ought to go to bed with her rough throat and her bad cough.
  Although there was a drought he felt he ought to water his garden.
  She bought some tough shoes for going through the rough ground.

Cross-curicular link

PSHE: thinking of others.

Swallow Journey

Enjoy this beautifully illustrated story, which is full of facts and a chance to think about more unusual spellings.

Suitable for

Children who are gaining confidence with spelling.

Aims

To introduce the children to the richness of their language as they use the French pronunciation of the grapheme 'our'.

Resources

- French, V. (2001) *Swallow Journey*, Slough: Zero to Ten Limited
- Individual books of plain paper made from eight sheets of A4 paper and a card cover

What to do

- Read and enjoy this story of a year in the life of a swallow.
- Explain to the children that they are to write a journal of the swallow's journey. Write this instruction on the whiteboard so that the children can see the two words, 'journey' and 'journal'. They are both based on the same French word, '*jour*'.
- Here is some background information which you may want to share with the children:
  '*journey*' has an unusual pronunciation of the grapheme 'our' – /j/ /ur/ /n/ /ee/.
  This pronunciation occurs in words of French origin where it is based on the word '*jour*', pronounced /zh/ /oo/ /ə/, which became '*journée*' or a day's travelling.
  It is also in '*journal*', which is a day-to-day record of events.

- Remind the children that, like a diary, a journal will contain lots of facts, times and places.
- Children can design their own cover with the title 'Journal of a journey'.
- Work on page one as a guided writing exercise. Ask the children in which month the story starts, and where the swallows are at that time: April, England. Form this into a sentence and ask the children to write it in their books. Page two can be a summary of the birds' summer, laying eggs and rearing their young.
- Page three is the autumn and the start of the journey. At this point read the book again, with the children noting down the places that the birds fly over.
- Complete the journal, using one page for each part of the journey:
    p.3 Cross English Channel to NW France
    p.4 Cross France and over the Pyrenees into Spain
    p.5 Cross Spain and over the sea to N Africa
    p.6 Cross the Sahara desert
    p.7 To South Africa
    p.8 In March leave for the return journey to England.
- Illustrations can be added later.

Variation

- Spend time with a globe or a world map plotting the swallows' journey.

Cross-curricular link

Geography: maps and journeys.

Castles

Exploit children's fascination with castles to practise words that end with 'le'.

Suitable for

Children who are gaining confidence with spelling.

Aims

To help children learn to spell the word 'castle' and other words with the same ending.

Resources

- Sims, L. (2002) *The Usborne Book of Castles*, London: Usborne Publishing Ltd

What to do

- Read and enjoy the book together.
- Ask the children to look at the word *'castle'* in the book title. Notice that the final phoneme is spelt with 'le'.
- How many words can the children suggest that have that ending? Suggestions might include: *little, circle, single, bottle, jungle, uncle, triangle, candle, bubble, middle, trouble, chuckle, wiggle.*
- Ask the children to make up sentences that include at least two words that end like 'castle', e.g.
    There is a castle in the middle of the jungle.
    Suddenly the candle blew out.
- Tick off the words when they have been used, to encourage variety.

- Then try making up a story about a castle, using these ideas to describe what happens. Ask the children to suggest a sentence at a time and see where it takes you! E.g.

  One day I went to visit my *uncle*. He lives in a *castle* in the *middle* of the *jungle*. My *uncle grumbled* because it was dark so he gave me a *single candle* and we went inside. I sat down while he put the *kettle* on. Suddenly I heard a *giggle* as a *bubble* floated by. My *little* cousin was blowing *bubbles* from a *bottle*. The *trouble* was that the *bubble* landed on the *candle*. Then we had a *chuckle* singing 'Hey *Diddle Diddle'* in the dark.

Variation

- Create a display of bubbles with a picture of something that ends with 'le' inside each bubble.

Cross-curricular link

English: words with a common spelling pattern.

A pocketful of rye

Use the rhyme 'Sing a song of sixpence' to create a game that practises adding the suffix 'ful' to a range of words.

Suitable for

Children who are gaining confidence with spelling.

Aims

To provide an opportunity for adding the suffix 'ful' to a range of words.

Resources

- A3 card
- Small pieces of paper to be decorated as pockets
- Words printed on cards: some that can have the suffix added, e.g. *pocket, hand, bag, truth, wonder, wish, hope, hate, spite, power, use, cheer, waste, faith, peace, thought*; and some that cannot, e.g. *sweet, worry, anger, light, smile, turn*
- Dice and counters

What to do

- Working with a small group of children, say the rhyme 'Sing a song of sixpence' together.
- Write the word *pocketful* on the board.
- Cover up the suffix 'ful' and ask the children to read the remaining word.
  Have the children got pockets? What might their pockets be 'full' of? (It may be appropriate to mention that the spelling changes to a single 'l' when it becomes a suffix.)
- Ask for ideas of other words that can have 'ful' added to them, and show the children the word cards and discuss the meanings of the words.

(It might be appropriate to consider the spelling of familiar words such as *beautiful* and *awful*.)

- Explain to the children that they are going to make a board game about making new words by adding the suffix '*ful*' to words.
- Help the children draw a number track across the A3 card and number it. They can then decorate the board with blackbirds.
- Ask them to decorate the squares of paper to make 'pockets' and glue these at intervals along the number track, obscuring some of the numbers.
- Explain to the children that if they land on a pocket they must pick up a word card.
  If the word they pick up can have '*ful*' added they keep the word.
  If '*ful*' cannot be added to the word they miss a go.
  If they pick up the word 'pocket' they have another go.
- Throw the dice and play the game. The game ends when there are no words left and the winner is the child with the most word cards.

Variation

- If you don't want to make the board game, simply pile the word cards in the middle of a small group of children. Ask them to take a word card in turn and play the game following the rules above.

Cross-curricular link

PSHE: taking turns.

Do You Want to be My Friend?

> Use the word *'want'* in the title of this book to explore the effect of 'w' on 'a'.

Suitable for

Children who are gaining confidence with spelling.

Aims

To help children learn that when 'a' follows 'w' it often sounds like /o/.

Resources

Carle, E. (1999) *Do You Want to be My Friend?*, London: Picture Puffins

What to do

- Read and enjoy the book together.
- Look at the title of the book and focus on the word *'want'*.
  Ask the children to segment the word and find the odd phoneme or sound.
- Cover up the 'w' and ask the children what the word reads now.
  Explain that often when a 'w' comes before an 'a' it changes the sound to /o/.
- Write *'ash'* on the board and ask the children to read the word.
- Then add a few different initial graphemes, e.g. *cash, flash, dash, mash*.
  Ask the children to read the words.
- Now add 'w' as the initial grapheme to make *'wash'*.
  Can the children read the word?
- Demonstrate with *'and'* in the same way, with *hand, band, stand*.
  Then ask them to add 'w' as the initial grapheme.
  How do we pronounce wand?
- Give the children the word *'catch'* and ask them to change the 'c' to a 'w'.
  What word have they made?

Variation

- Play a team game with the word-endings *ant, ash, and, atch*.

  (It might be appropriate to include '*at*' since '*what*' contains an 'a' for the phoneme /o/ even though it's written with 'wh'.)

  Give each team one of the word-endings then call out an initial phoneme. If the team can make a word with that phoneme they raise their hand. One member is chosen to say the word. Every correct word gets a point. The first team to six points wins.

  Words can be made with the following initial phonemes:

  ash – b, c, d, f+l, m, w
  and – b, h, l, s, s+t, w
  at – b, c, f, f+l, h, m, w
  ant – ch, p, p+l, s+l, w
  atch – c, h, l, m, p, w

Cross-curricular link

English: spelling.

Part 2
Illustrating phonics

Chapter 5
Stage A

Cats with curly tails

> Everyone makes a collage cat or kitten and thinks up a name for them.

Suitable for

Children who are practising single-letter sounds.

Aims

To help children use and recognise the phoneme /k/.

Resources

- Farjeon, E. (2009) *Cats Sleep Anywhere*, London: Frances Lincoln Publishers Ltd
- Scissors, paper, glue, crayons and embossed wallpaper

What to do

- Tell the children to listen to the instructions and count how many /k/ sounds they can hear. 'Carefully colour and cut out a collage cat or kitten with a curly tail.'
  It might be appropriate to write the instructions for the children – use a different-coloured pen to highlight the /k/ phonemes in the sentence.
- Show the children how to use the crayons to make a rubbing from the embossed wallpaper to create a pattern suitable for representing fur.
- Explain that the body and head of the cat can be cut out of this paper.
- Demonstrate how to curl a strip of paper around a pencil to make a curly tail.
- As the children make their cat or kitten, keep repeating the instructions.

- Encourage the children to use as many words as they can beginning with /k/ sounds when they show their finished pictures to the other children during a show-and-tell session.
- Display the cats and kittens with a caption – *Can you carefully cut and colour a cat or kitten with a curly tail?*
- Read the poem 'Cats Sleep Anywhere' by Eleanor Farjeon to the children.

Variation

- The children could now choose a name beginning with the same sound and write or copy the word to be displayed with their cat or kitten.
  E.g. *Clara, Kevin, Chris, Candy, Kiera, Katy, Coco.*

Cross-curricular link

Science: living things.

Funny fish

Fill in a picture outline with alliterative words and phrases.

Suitable for

Children who are practising single-letter sounds.

Aims

To encourage children to recall and write words that begin with the sound /f/.

Resources

- Picture dictionaries
- Some pictures of fish or toy fish
- Paper and coloured pencils or felt-tip pens
- Cardboard templates of fish – optional

What to do

- Spend some time looking at the fish pictures or toys. Encourage the children to talk about their shapes and the position of their fins and eyes.
- How many appropriate words can they find that begin with /f/? E.g. *funny, fancy, five, fluffy, four, friendly, fantastic, flowery.*
- The children are going to write inside the outline of a fish. Some of your children may be able to draw a large enough fish to do this. If not, use some templates that you have prepared. Show the children how to use some removable adhesive to hold it in place on a piece of paper while they draw round it. They can then remove the template to reveal the shape.

- The children should now write some of their /f/ words inside the fish outline, following the shape. You may need to demonstrate this first. Use pens in bright colours for the writing and the outline.
- The fish can be cut out and mounted onto a display board that has layers of blue/green tissue paper stuck across it to represent the sea, or an aquarium. Add some green strips for weeds.

Variation

- Use other themes for other phonemes, e.g.
  - A butterfly outline and words about mini-beasts
  - A pear outline and words describing fruit
  - A light-bulb outline and words about electricity

Cross-curricular link

Science: living things.

A *zoo* plan

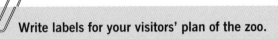

Write labels for your visitors' plan of the zoo.

Suitable for

Children who are practising their single-letter sounds.

Aims

To reinforce the children's knowledge of the /d/ phoneme and grapheme.

Resources

- A prepared plan that includes a lake, a large tree and some pens/enclosures and pathways
- Copies of this plan for the children to use or A3 paper for them to make their own if time is available
- Cards with the name and a picture of things beginning with /d/, e.g. *dog, dinosaur, dragon, dragonfly, donkey, dove, dolphin, deer, dingo, dormouse, duck, dalmation* – and *Daddy!*

What to do

- Explain to the children that they are to set up an imaginary zoo for children to visit. It's a very strange zoo because all the animals in it have to be called something beginning with /d/.
- Encourage the children to make some suggestions. Have the cards ready in case they struggle. Now hand out the cards, so that everyone has one. Who can show you an animal that lives in water, or in a tree, or in a secret quiet place, and so on? The children should hold their card up if they think they have this sort of animal.
- Now collect all the cards back in and stick them up on a wall, or lay them on a spare table so that the children can use them to copy the words later.

- Show the children the outline plan that you have prepared. What sort of places are there on it?
  Talk about the lake, the tree and the different-sized enclosures.
- Explain to the children that the plan is to help visitors to find their way around the zoo to their favourite animal. The children need to decide where each animal will be and write its name in that place. They should think carefully about the best places for the different animals.
- If time is available, children could draw the animals, add other details and colour it all in. They could choose a name for their zoo. Will it begin with /d/?

Variation

- Children could make up some sentences about the animals using words from their plan, e.g.

  The dragonfly likes to be near the water.
  The dove lives in the tree.

Cross-curricular link

Geography: map-making.

What's in Santa's sack?

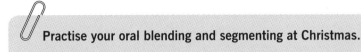

Practise your oral blending and segmenting at Christmas.

Suitable for

Children who are practising single-letter sounds.

Aims

To encourage the children to listen carefully to the phonemes in words.

Resources

- A large Christmas sack or pillow case
- A selection of items with your chosen phoneme as their initial sound, e.g. *rabbit, roundabout, ring, robin, ruler, ribbon, rubber, rose, rat, rag-doll, raisins*
- Paper, crayons, laminator
- Large label

What to do

- 'Find' the sack when you come into the classroom after a break. What can it be? Who does it belong to? It must have dropped from Santa's sleigh!
- Gather the children round you whilst you reveal the presents one by one. Hold one of the presents inside the sack so that the children can't see. Tell them 'It's a ...'.
- Sound out each phoneme in its name slowly and clearly. Remember to always use pure sounds when you do this so that you don't add any unwanted sounds that would confuse the children. Look at Appendix 1 on pages 326–7 for more advice on this.
- Once the children have worked out what it is, show it to them and help them to segment its name.

- Continue until all the presents are out of the sack. Did the children notice anything about these things? Accept their ideas until they recognise that they all started with the same phoneme.
- Children could come out one at a time and have a go at reaching into the sack and segmenting the name of their chosen present for others to identify. The presents could be replaced in the sack each time in case someone needs the confidence boost of repeating something they have just heard.
- Children choose one present each (or something else beginning with /r/) to illustrate. They can draw and colour it before cutting it out, ready to be laminated.
- Ask the children if they know who the lucky child is who is going to be given the sack of presents. It has to be someone whose name also starts with the phoneme /r/ – perhaps it will be Rebecca, or Rashid, or Richard? Come to an agreement with the children and write that name on the label and attach it to the sack.
- Put the children's pictures into the sack and leave it near your Christmas tree. Perhaps they will play guess the present and practise their oral blending and segmenting.

Variation

- Make three or four stockings and hang them onto a display board that represents a mantelpiece. On each stocking place a name label. Children could be given the task of choosing, drawing and cutting out an object for one stocking. It should start with the same phoneme as the name on one of the stockings. Where will they place it?

Cross-curricular link

RE: giving, festivals.

Sliding sounds

Help the children make this sliding strip of sounds to change the word.

Suitable for

Children who are practising single-letter sounds.

Aims

To help children use oral blending and segmenting skills.

Resources

- Template of a simple cat picture
- A piece of card and separate strip of card for each child

What to do

- Working with a small group, show the children the template of the cat and help them draw around it and cut it out.
- Now cut two slits horizontally across the cat's tummy so that the card strip fits in and slides up and down.

- Ask the children to segment the word '*cat*' and help them write the word on their cat across the strip.
  Write the first letter on the strip and the last two letters on the cat.
- Now show them how to slide the strip up so there is an empty space before the 'at'.
- Ask the children to write a 'h' on the strip next to the 'at'. Can they read the new word?
- Ask for other words that have the same ending as '*cat*' and '*hat*'.
- Encourage the children to write the initial letters *r, f, m, s* on the sliding strip to create *rat, fat, mat, sat*.
- The children will enjoy sliding the strip and reading their words.

Variation

- This is a useful tool when you are practising words where the vowel sound is changed by the final 'e'. E.g. write the word *ake* on a picture of a cake. Then add the initial letters *c, m, r, l, t, b, w* to the sliding strip in front of these letters. The words *cake, make, rake, lake, take, bake, wake* can now be read.
- Or use a paper plate with a sliding strip. Write the two initial consonants '*pl*' on the sliding strip and the ending 'ate' on the plate. Then add the initials *l, d, g, f, h, m, sl, sk, st* to the sliding strip to create the words *late, date, gate, fate, hate, slate, skate, state*.

Cross-curricular link

DT: joining materials.

Planet X

Be the master of your own universe.

Suitable for

Children who are practising single-letter sounds.

Aims

To help the children hear and write the letter 'x'.

Resources

- Sand tray
- A selection of small cardboard boxes, tubes, etc.
- Oddments of cardboard and felt-tip pens
- Flat lolly sticks

What to do

- Tell the children that they are going to make a model of an imaginary planet called Planet X.
  This is a strange planet where every place, every person, everything that you can get to eat – absolutely everything – has the letter 'x' somewhere in it.
- The planet is going to be in the sand tray. The children can mound up the sand to make an interesting surface for your planet. Mark some features in it, e.g. a hill and a crater.
- Ask the children what they think they should be called. This is a good activity for encouraging the children to make up their own words, e.g. *Mount Bix* or *the crater of Tux*.
- Write some labels for these with the children helping by sounding out the words and identifying the letters you should use. Place the labels on the hill and in the crater.

- Tell the children that they need some aliens to live on their planet, and the aliens will need houses. Children can work together to draw, colour and cut out some cardboard aliens before sticking them onto the lolly sticks. They will then be able to make them stand up in the sand. They can then use the boxes and tubes to make a house for each alien they have made. The children should make their own label 'This is …'s house'. All of their aliens should have an 'x' in their name, e.g. *Dixi, Hax, Moox, Sloxy, Woxa.*
- Place these in the sand tray and leave them for the children to enjoy.

Variation

- Children could add other features as they play.
  Leave paper and pencils nearby and encourage the children to draw their own maps of Planet X.

Cross-curricular link

Geography: places.

The pottery shop

Make some pottery ornaments from clay and set up a shop.

Suitable for

Children who are practising single-letter sounds.

Aims

To provide an opportunity for the children to practise the /o/ phoneme in reading and spelling.

Resources

- Clay and paint, with optional varnish
- Classroom shop, with money
- Card for labels
- Paper for shopping lists

What to do

- Explain to the children that they are going to set up a pottery shop. To do this they will need to have some pottery to sell. They are to make this using clay.
- This shop can only sell things with an /o/ sound in them. What might they sell? If possible, show the children some ornaments made from pottery to help them think of ideas. Or just use pictures. These may suggest *frog, donkey, doll, log, fox, dog, spotted plate, cot, clock, (tea) pot, cod, sock, lock, box, chop, top*.
- Once these items are made, dried and painted they are ready to go in the shop.
- Spend time segmenting the names of the items and helping the children to work out the spelling, drawing attention to the 'o' grapheme.

- Then the children can make price labels with the name of the item and the price on it. Attach these to the items by punching a hole in the card and threading some cord or string through, before tying it on.
- Alternatively, you could make a large price list to fix up in the shop. Work with the group of children to segment and then spell each item. Then choose children to write up each item in turn, with its price.
- Make a large name for your Pottery Shop, set everything out attractively and it is ready for play.
- Children can write out their shopping list and pay for their goods in the usual way.

Variation

- Everybody could make a traditional pot and decorate it with painted spots and dots, or dogs, frogs, etc.

Cross-curricular link

Maths: using money.

Five little bees

Make a display of a hive and bees as you practise this buzzzzzzzzing rhyme.

Suitable for

Children who are practising single-letter sounds.

Aims

To say the /z/ phoneme and practise writing the grapheme 'z'.

Resources

- A display board covered in light-blue paper
- A hexagon template and strong paper
- Cardboard tubes, yellow, black and white tissue paper

What to do

- Explain to the children that bees build a honeycomb inside their hive, and each separate part of the honeycomb is a six-sided shape called a hexagon. Show them the template. They are to draw round the template, colour it in using any shades of yellow or orange and then cut it out.
- All the templates can be stuck to the display to represent the honeycomb.
- Children can make bees by wrapping strips of yellow and black tissue round a tube. Next, fold a sheet of white tissue in half, crush it up and then glue it at the central crease onto the tube to make the wings.
- What sound do bees make? They buzz. Who can write a 'z'? Show the children how they can write lots of 'z's together to make a bee sound.

- Now learn this poem together.
  Five children should be chosen to sit on the floor and be the bees.
  They can hold their model bees.
  At the word 'buzzzzzz' one child will stand up and make their bee fly away.

  Five little bees buzzing on the floor
  Buzzzzzz and that leaves four
  Four little bees buzzing by the tree
  Buzzzzzz and that leaves three
  Three little bees buzzing on my shoe
  Buzzzzzz and that leaves two
  Two little bees buzzing in the sun
  Buzzzzzz and that leaves one
  One little bee buzzing near the hive
  Buzzzzzz and now there are five.

- When you have finished with the rhyme the bees can be fixed to the display along with the words of the rhyme.

Variation

- Make a display illustrating each part of the rhyme – five bees on the floor, etc.

Cross-curricular link

Maths: shapes.

In the garden

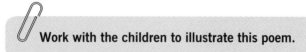

Work with the children to illustrate this poem.

Suitable for

Children who are practising single-letter sounds.

Aims

To concentrate on words that start with the /g/ phoneme.

Resources

- Paint, paper and other collage materials

What to do

- Read the poem with the children.

    It's gloomy in Grandpa's shed
    Where there's a pot of gunky glue
    A grizzly bug
    A grimy goal post
    A gardening glove
    A grotty guitar
    And probably – a ghost.

    It's gorgeous in Granny's garden
    Where there's a golden sunflower
    A great big apple tree
    A gooseberry bush
    A green grassy lawn
    A garden hose
    And probably – a girl in a glittery gown.

- Can the children count how many /g/ sounds there are? Read it again, slowly, so that they can count.

- Ask the children to think about all the things in the shed. Can they remember some of the 'g' words, e.g. *gloomy, grimy, gunky, grotty*. Compare these words to the ones used to describe the things in the garden, e.g. *golden, great, glittery*.
- Cover the left half of a display board in a dark paper to look like the gloomy shed. Cover the other half in green and blue to represent the garden.
- Children can now choose one item from the lists to paint or collage. Cut out the finished pictures and attach them to the board, either in the shed or in the garden.
- Use the first line of each verse as a title for each half. Children can copy the line they illustrated onto card and fix it near their picture. Use this writing as a chance to focus on the correct way to form the letter 'g' and position it appropriately alongside the other letters.

Variation

- Children could each work on a smaller piece of paper folded in half, to illustrate their personal copy of the poem.

Cross-curricular link

English: vocabulary development.

Vicky's village shop

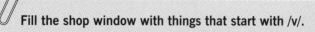

Fill the shop window with things that start with /v/.

Suitable for

Children who are practising single-letter sounds.

Aims

To encourage the children to listen for the sound /v/ at the start of words.

Resources

- Cut out a cardboard shop front with a large window – just a space – and a door that will open; fix it to a display board
  Cut a piece of card to fit exactly its width for the shop name; this will be fitted onto the board, above the shop
- A shopping bag full of objects, most of them starting with the sound /v/, e.g. *a book about a volcano with a clear picture of this on the cover, a vest, a video, a vase, a bottle of vinegar, an empty tub for vanilla ice-cream, clearly marked as such, a van, some vegetables,* or *a tin of vegetable soup*
  Add a few things that don't start with /v/ to create a challenge

What to do

- Tell the children that on the display board is a picture of a village shop. The shop is run by Vicky (or any other name beginning with /v/).
- Show the children the card for the shop name and tell them that you need to write *Vicky's Village Shop* on it. Ask them to help you sound out the words as you write it. Fix it in place.
- Explain to the children that Vicky only sells things that begin with the same sound as her name. Can anyone tell you what that is?
- Now show them your bag of shopping. Which things did you buy from Vicky's shop?

- Choose one child to reach into the bag and take something out. Ask them to identify it and then decide whether it starts with /v/ or not. If you bought it at Vicky's shop put it in one pile. If not, make a second pile.
- Choose a second child to pick something from your bag. Continue until all your goods are sorted.
- The children can now make drawings of things that Vicky might sell and fix them in her shop window. Add labels with the letter 'v' in a bold colour each time it occurs.

Variation

- This activity can easily be used with any initial sound simply by changing the name above the shop. Try, *Tom's town stores, Sally's supermarket, Mary's market stall, William's web page.*

Cross-curricular link

Geography: the place where we live.

Chapter 6
Stage B

A bird's eye view

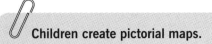 Children create pictorial maps.

Suitable for

Children who are learning graphemes with more than one letter.

Aims

To provide an opportunity for children to read and write words with the /ar/ phoneme when it is written only as 'ar'.

Resources

- Story books with pictorial maps, e.g. those by Richard Scarry, or any word books that contain labelled pictorial maps
- Individual word cards of /ar/ words, e.g. *car, car park, supermarket, market, park, star, scarf, cardigan, bar, farm, farmhouse, cart, barn*
  Beware of 'garage' – the /a/ and /r/ are individual phonemes in this word

What to do

- Children can work in pairs or small groups to do this activity.
- Distribute the word cards to the pairs/groups of children. They should read them to each other and then swap cards with another pair/group.
- Collect the cards in and very quickly let the children read each one out loud as you hold them up.
- Explain to the children that they are going to create a pictorial map of a village that is next to a farm.
- Show them some pictorial maps, and leave the books available for them to access them as they work.
- They should draw their map on a large sheet of paper and then add labels, using as many of the /ar/ words as possible. Remind them that they can always label things in shop windows.

Variation

- Children could write some sentences including words from their map to form a descriptive piece of writing.

Cross-curricular link

Geography: maps.

The queue

> The children make up some quiz questions about their display.

Suitable for

Children who are learning graphemes with more than one letter.

Aims

To encourage children to use the 'wh' question words in a fun context.

Resources

- A display that has been created beforehand:
  At one side of the board have a bus stop sign. Draw round children of
  differing heights to make some figures to stand in your queue. Add features
  in a collage style. You might be able to use some old clothes and staple them
  on. Aim to have a wide variety of people, with identifiable roles, e.g.

  a mummy with a buggy and baby
  an elderly person with a shopping bag
  a business person with an umbrella and briefcase or a laptop
  a teenager in school uniform
  an old man with his dog
  a lady with a cat basket
  someone carrying a violin case
  a child with a football
  a child with a present or a balloon

What to do

- Explain to the children that they are going to be making up some
  questions. Can they tell you the words that usually start questions?

  What? Who? When? Why? Where?

  Point out to the children that 'who' begins with the same grapheme
  but a different phoneme: /h/.

- Write them down and ask the children what they all begin with. They should be aware that the two letters 'w' and 'h' make the one sound /wh/.
- Write the five words on the whiteboard and ask the children for some suggestions about a question that starts with the first word on your list, e.g.

    Who is first in the queue?

  Continue through all the five question words, e.g.
    Where is the teenager going?
    What's in the old man's shopping bag?
    When is the bus due to arrive?
    Why is the lady in the suit carrying an umbrella?

- Tell them that they are now going to work with a partner to make up five questions of their own about the people in the bus queue. They should start by writing out the five question starter words, spaced out down the page. When they have completed their questions they should swap papers with another pair of children and try to answer their questions.

Variation

- Use the 'who' word in a mathematical context, e.g.

    Who is third in the queue?
    Who is the tallest person?
    Who is next to the teenager?
    Who is standing between the mummy and the old man?

Cross-curricular link

Maths: ordering.

Make a bookmark

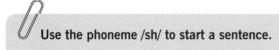

Use the phoneme /sh/ to start a sentence.

Suitable for

Children who are learning graphemes of more than one letter.

Aims

To give the children an opportunity for writing and reading the phoneme /sh/.

Resources

- Strips of card 15cm long
- Felt-tip pens and scissors

What to do

- Work with a small group of children around a table.
- Ask them what it means when someone puts their finger to their lips and says /sh/ – demonstrate this.
- Write the word on the board and explain why an exclamation mark is used.
  Discuss why or when you would say this to someone.
- Then ask for ideas to finish this sentence:
  'Shhh! I'm trying to ...'
- The children might suggest: *read, think, sleep, sing, listen, watch, work, write, speak*.
- Tell the children they are going to make a bookmark and therefore the most appropriate sentence probably is:
  'Shhh! I'm trying to read'.
- Show them how to write the word **Shhh!** in large bold letters along the strip of card, leaving a space at the end of the word.
- Punch a hole in the card at the opposite end.

- Then turn the card over and write the rest of the sentence on the reverse of the bookmark.

- Use a piece of thick coloured wool to make a tassel through the hole.

Variation

- You could let the children write their suggestions for the ending of the sentence on individual whiteboards. This would provide an opportunity for you to assess their spelling of a range of words that include a variety of graphemes.

Cross-curricular link

DT: focused practical task.

Find the squares

Inspire the children to create their own Mondrian pictures and label the squares.

Suitable for

Children who are learning graphemes of more than one letter.

Aims

To give the children an opportunity to write the grapheme 'qu'.

Resources

- Drawing program on the computer, or paper, thick felt-tip pens and rulers
- Copy of *Composition* by Mondrian
- Card labels with the word 'square' printed on each one
- Blu-Tack

What to do

- Show the children a reproduction of the Mondrian picture.
- Ask the children how they think the artist created this composition. Discuss the straight black lines that create a grid pattern.
  Notice how some sections are coloured with vivid primary colours.
- Ask the children how many squares they can see.
  Notice that some squares are coloured and some are still white.
  You may also want to remind the children of the difference between squares and rectangles.
- Show the children one of the labels that reads *square*.
  Can the children show you which letters represent the /kw/ phoneme?
  (The phoneme represented by 'qu' is technically two phonemes – /k/ /w/ – but it is more simple to teach this as one sound with young children.)

- Can anyone suggest some other words with this phoneme, e.g. *quiz, quick, queen, question, squash, squirt.*
  Let the children take turns to stick the labels onto the square shapes on the Mondrian.
  Now show the children how to create their own version:
  - by either drawing black lines with felt-tip pens and ruler and colouring in some sections;
  - or by using a drawing program on the computer to create a grid pattern, then filling some sections with colour.
- Let the children label the squares on their artwork with detachable labels.

Variation

- The children could count how many squares they have created with their grid pattern and write this on strips of paper for display below their artwork.

Cross-curricular link

Art and design: investigating work by different artists.

Whaam

Help the children paint their own version of this painting with 'made-up' words.

Suitable for

Children who are learning graphemes of more than one letter.

Aims

To encourage children to use their phonic knowledge to spell invented words.

Resources

- A copy of *Whaam* by Roy Lichenstein
- Thick felt-tip pens, paints and paper

What to do

- Look at the painting together. Read the words in the pilot's speech bubble and segment the noise word. Is this a real word? Why is it there?
- Explain that the artist wanted to make his paintings look like a printed comic – help them notice the drawing style of the plane and flames, the limited range of colours, the use of speech bubbles and printed words describing noise.
- Ask the children to think of another exciting event, e.g.
  a ball hitting the back of the goal
  a fire engine or police car speeding by
  a wizard casting a spell
  lightning hitting a tree in a storm.
- Then discuss ideas for the sound effects of each event.
  Help the children create invented words for these noises: *deedah, wheeeee, kaplunk*.
- Write their ideas for made-up sound effects on the board.

- Let the children draw out their compositions.
- Ask them to write a speech or 'thought' bubble that describes what's happening in the picture, e.g.
  The traffic stopped as the police car drove by.
  (It may be appropriate for the children to work in pairs on these pictures.)
- Display the children's paintings on a background of collaged newspaper and comics.

Variation

- Collect together a list of exciting incidents that can be described with sound effects, then let children take turns inventing a word for the sound effect and writing it on the board. Can the children match the sound effect to the incident?

Cross-curricular link

Art: investigating work by different artists.

Owls

> The children make their own owls and then work together to create a poem.

Suitable for

Children who are learning graphemes of more than one letter.

Aims

To reinforce the spelling of the phoneme /oo/.

Resources

- Brown paper bags
- Scrap tissue paper
- Paint and brushes
- Collage paper for eyes, claws and beak

What to do

- Look together at pictures of owls.
- Paint the flat brown paper bags to look like the feathers of an owl and leave them to dry.
- Next day, talk about owl sounds: *Tu-whit-tu-whoo, hoot-hoot, whoo-hoo*. Ask the children to think of some other words that have this sound, e.g. *moon, soon, food, mood, cool, pool, swoop, roof, hoop, loop*.
- As the children stuff their paper-bag owls with screwed up tissue paper, ask them to make up sentences or phrases about their owl using the /oo/ words.

Some suggestions:

The owl flies in a loop across the silver moon.
Mummy owl swoops down with food.
High on the roof, daddy owl hoots.
An owl whooshes over the cool pool.

- Staple the bags closed then add claws, eyes and a beak.
- Display the owls perched on a branch with a dark-blue background covered in silver stars and a large crescent moon.
- Use the children's phrases to make a poem. This can then be added to the display.

Variation

- Make speech bubbles for each owl. Let the children write a sentence or phrase for their owl's speech bubble using a word with the phoneme /oo/. E.g. *hoot-hoot, tu-whit-tu-whoo, see you soon, here comes food, stay cool, fly over the moon, perch on the roof.*

Cross-curricular link

English: speech bubbles.

Wood and wool

As children make sculptures using these two materials they become aware of words with the grapheme 'oo' creating the phoneme /u/.

Suitable for

Children who are learning graphemes of more than one letter.

Aims

To provide an opportunity for children to focus on the grapheme 'oo'.

Resources

- Small branches and twigs from trees
- A selection of different-coloured wools

What to do

- If possible, collect some small branches or twigs with the children. (If not, allow the children to handle the ones you've brought in.)
- Show the children the different-coloured wool that they are going to use to make their sculptures.
- Before the children start work on their sculptures ask them to segment the words *wood* and *wool*.
- Explain that these words use 'oo' to make the /u/ sound, or phoneme.
  (Be sensitive to local accents and how this affects their pronunciation.)
- Tell the children that *look* also has 'oo' in the middle and that a good way to remember this is to give the word eyes so it can look!
- Write the word *look* on the board and draw two little eyes in the 'oo'.
- Then write *wood* and *wool* before choosing two children to make eyes on them.
  Tell them this will remind them that these words have the same middle sound as *look*.

- Write more examples on the board and ask the children to read them: *hook, took, cook, book, shook, hood, good, blood, stood.* Let children who read the words add eyes to them on the board. (It may be appropriate to explain that other words with the grapheme 'oo' create the phoneme /oo/.)
- Now start creating your sculptures:
  - Help the children knot the wool to the branch then show them how to wind the wool across the spaces between the twigs.
  - A child or an adult needs to hold the branch while the child winds the wool, and several children can take turns decorating one branch.
  - If you are using separate twigs, make a simple framework by binding them together with wool, then help the children wind the wool across the spaces to create individual sculptures.
  - Or let the children wind wool around individual twigs or pieces of wood to create simple bands of various colours.
- Display the sculptures together with a title:
  Look at our wool and wood sculptures
  Don't forget to add eyes to the 'oo' graphemes in the three words!

Variation

- Ask the children to make a collection of items made of wood or wool and display them together with words that share this grapheme.

Cross-curricular link

Science: materials and their properties.

Phonic wheel

Children enjoy making these wheels and using them to practise reading words.

Suitable for

Children who are learning graphemes of more than one letter.

Aims

To help children use oral blending skills when reading new words.

Resources

- Two card circles for each wheel, one smaller and one larger
- Brass fasteners

What to do

- Working with a small group, show the children how to assemble their wheel. Lay the smaller circle on top of the larger one and fix the brass fastener in the centre through both circles so the wheels turn.
- Remind the children of an initial sound that you have been learning e.g. 'ch'.
- Show the children how to write the grapheme on the outer edge of the smaller inner circle.

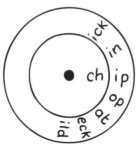

- Think of a few simple words that begin with that sound, e.g. *chip, chin, chick, chat, chap, chop, chink, check, child*.
- Write one of these on the board, separating the initial grapheme, i.e. 'ch', from the ending of the word. Read the word together.
- Help each child to write a different ending on the outer circle next to the initial grapheme so they can all read a different word on their wheel.
- Now show them how to turn their outer wheel a little so they can write another word-ending against the initial grapheme. Read the new words.
- When the children have written six or seven words the wheels are complete.
  The children will enjoy playing with their wheels and reading aloud the words they can make.

Variation

- This is a useful tool for practising consonant blends at the beginning of words. Ensure that the children realise they are writing two phonemes on the inner circle, e.g. 'bl', then proceed in the same way by adding word-endings to the outer circle to create words, e.g. *black, blink, blob, blend, blast, blink, bless*.

Cross-curricular link

DT: assembling and joining.

A whole lot of holes

Make an art collection of holes and use the opportunity to develop their phonic skills.

Suitable for

Children who are learning graphemes of more than one letter.

Aims

To develop children's understanding of the split diagraph 'o-e'.

Resources

- Camera
- White paper circles of varying sizes
- Felt-tip pens

What to do

- Write the word 'hole' on the board.
  Ask the children if anyone can read the word.
  Tell them the word says 'hole'.
- Cover up the final letter 'e' and read the rest of the word
  (pronounced as the beginning of 'holiday').
  Explain that the 'e' on the end makes the letter 'o' say /oa/.
- Demonstrate other words where the /oa/ phoneme is created by the
  letter 'e'. E.g. *bone, cone, home, nose, rose, pole, mole, joke*.
- Ask the children to think of where they have seen a hole.
  Ideas might include: the back of a chair, a mint sweet, a doughnut,
  in a tree, a buttonhole, on buttons, scissors, an animal skull.
- Take a small group of children out with a camera to photograph
  some of their ideas.

- Encourage everyone to write the word *hole* with brightly coloured felt-tip pens on circles of white paper.
- Display the photographs and the white circles on a black backing paper to create *a whole lot of holes* and use this phrase as the title.
- It might be appropriate to explain that the words *whole* and *hole* sound the same but have different meanings and are spelt differently.

Variation

- Using white paper, cut out several of each of the four letters in the word *hole* using large letter templates. Let the children work in pairs to make holes in their four letters with a hole punch and then glue the letters in the correct order on brightly coloured pieces of paper to form the word. Display the children's work using the title of the activity.

Cross-curricular link

Art and design: using materials and tools.

Chapter 7
Stage C

Let's Dance

Use the painting *The Dance* by Matisse to focus on words with the grapheme 'ce'.

Suitable for

Children who are learning alternative graphemes.

Aims

To raise children's awareness of the grapheme 'ce' for the phoneme /s/.

Resources

- A copy of *The Dance* by Matisse
- Music for dancing

What to do

- Show the children a reproduction of the painting.
- Ask the children what's happening in the picture.
- Play the music and dance together in a circle.
  Ask the children to think what they are doing with their arms and legs as they dance.
- To help them appreciate the movement of the dance, ask two or three children to sit in the circle as the class dances around them.
- *The Dance* is a huge painting (260 x 391cm). Look at the painting again. Tell the children how large the painting is and ask them why the artist made it so big.
  Perhaps he wanted to involve the viewer in the dance?
- Write the title of the painting on the board and segment the word *dance*: d-a-n-ce.
  Notice how the final phoneme /s/ is written.

- Ask if the children can think of words that rhyme with *dance*.
  List their suggestions: *chance, prance, France*.
  Notice that all the words end with the grapheme 'ce'.
- Write another word that follows the same spelling pattern and ask
  them to think of a word that rhymes. E.g.
  - nice – ice
  - mice – rice
  - face – lace
  - space – place
  - pence – fence
  - since – prince.
  Erase all the words listed before the next part of the game.
- Let the children dance again but when the music stops choose
  someone to come to the board and write one of the words that ends
  with the same grapheme as dance – 'ce'.
- Continue dancing until you have listed 10 words.
  Perhaps the children would like to chant the words as they dance!

Variation

- Ask the children to get into small groups of four or five and give them a
  whiteboard to share. Tell the children they can dance with their group but
  when the music stops they have to write a word that ends with the grapheme
  'ce' on their whiteboard. Continue until they have listed 10 words.

Cross-curricular link

PE: dance activities.

The snail trail

Everyone can make a snail to slither round the trail.

Suitable for

Children who are learning alternative graphemes.

Aims

To raise the children's awareness of the variety of ways in which they could spell the /ai/ phoneme.

Resources

- Cut-out cardboard snail models that the children have made earlier
- Toys from farms, train sets, etc., that have an /ai/ phoneme in them, e.g. *a gate, railings, railtrack, train, station, crane, spade, window frame*
- Large sheet of sugar paper
- Tube of glitter glue

What to do

- A group of children should be sitting round a table or in a circle on the floor. Show them the toys and encourage them to name each one. Lay these out on the sugar paper in the middle of the group of children.
- Take one of the snails and decide where its 'home' is. Now explain that the snail is going to go to the station to meet his granny and then back to his home again. Ask the children to help you to describe its route as you move the snail round the trail, e.g.

  One day the snail went through the gate, down the lane, in front of the station, along the railtrack and all the way back home again.

- Children take it in turns to move their snail around the objects on the sugar paper whilst another child follows them with the glitter glue marking the snail's trail.
- Now write down your description of the route for the children, asking for their help with the spelling as you do so. Read it together.
- Ask the children if they can point to the words that rhyme with snail – the ones with the /ai/ sound in them. Encourage them to notice the different ways that it is written: 'ay', 'a-e', 'ai', 'a'.
- Children have a go at making up their own routes, and describing them to the group.

Variation

- Less able children could create a simple sentence each, limited to the 'ai' grapheme, e.g.

  The snail went to Spain. The snail went on a train. The snail went on a train to Spain.

Cross-curricular link

Geography: routes and following directions.

Night in the town

Encourage the children to use their sense of hearing to describe a night-time scene.

Suitable for

Children who are learning alternative graphemes.

Aims

To remind the children about the three ways in which they could read/say the 'ch' grapheme.

Resources

- Pictures of towns at night
- Sentences on individual cards, (see below)
- A selection of instruments

What to do

- Look at the pictures of towns at night. Talk about the children's own experiences of being outside at night.
- Talk about the fact that it is hard to see and that we may have to rely on hearing things.
- Write sentences on individual cards of things that you may hear in a town at night:

    The clock chiming on the church tower.
    Machines rumbling to a halt in the factory.
    The old chapel bells ringing out.
    The final click of the lock as the chemist's shop door closes.
    Christmas carols being sung by the school choir.
    The birds chirping as they settle down to roost.

- Ask the children to pick out the 'ch' graphemes and say them out loud. What do they notice? They can be pronounced in three different ways: as a soft /sh/, a hard /k/ or as /ch/.

- You might want to explain the reasons for this:
  In Greek, 'ch' is pronounced /k/. In French it is pronounced /sh/ and in Old English it is pronounced /ch/. So can they now tell you where each of these 'ch' words comes from?
- Provide a selection of instruments. Can the children choose some to represent each of the sentences about night-time? They can then spend some time in small groups devising a sound picture of the town at night.

Variation

- If it is inappropriate to have so many church/chapel/Christmas words in your class, use this activity of sounds at night attached to alternative phoneme/grapheme teaching points. Try:

  Mosque: use the phoneme /k/ and the grapheme 'qu'.
  Temple: use the grapheme /le/ for word-endings compared with 'el'.

Cross-curricular link

RE: places of worship.

Once upon a time

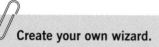 **Create your own wizard.**

Suitable for

Children who are learning alternative graphemes.

Aims

To use the children's imagination as they collect graphemes for the phoneme /oa/.

Resources

- Paper, pencils and paint

What to do

- Read this description to the children:

    A long time ago lived an old, old wizard who always wore an aubergine-coloured robe that reached from his shoulders to the tips of his toes. Over this robe he wore a cloak woven from threads of gold. This cloak had been sewn in the middle of the night by the fairy folk who lived among the roots of the great oak tree.

- Point out to the children that there are lots of /oa/ sounds. Can they hear them when you read it again? Ask them to put their hands up every time they hear this phoneme.
- Ask the children if they can tell you any more words with an /oa/ phoneme. Write the children's suggestions on the whiteboard. Now ask them to collate them by grapheme. How many lists will they have? We suggest:

    oa – coat
    ow – bowl
    ol – yolk

ou – shoulder
au – aubergine
oo – brooch
o – go
oh – doh
ough – although
oe – toe
ew – sew
o-e – bone

- Give each child a photocopy of the words of the story. They can stick this onto a piece of paper and then draw their interpretation of the wizard underneath.

Variation

- The children could continue the story of the wizard, describing some of the things he can do when he is wearing his magic golden cloak. Encourage them to include some more of the /oa/ words they have collected together.

Cross-curricular link

English: story writing.

One morning

Practise building complex sentences to tell your spider's adventure.

Suitable for

Children who are learning alternative graphemes.

Aims

To develop the children's creative writing skills as they practise using the /or/ phoneme and its many graphemes.

Resources

- A spider made from black card, white and black sticky paper eyes and a black thread

What to do

- Ask the children to work with a partner to find three alternative ways of spelling /or/. They could use:

  or – for
  our – four
  aw – draw
  awer – drawer
  oor – floor
  oar – board
  a – hall.

- Write up their ideas where everyone can see them.
- Write the simple starter sentence: *Paul saw a spider.*
- Now ask the children questions and add their responses to your sentence, making it longer and more complex each time.

- You could ask:

  When? *Early one morning, on Tuesday morning,*
      ... Early one morning Paul saw a spider.

  What was it doing? *Crawling, drawing, falling.*
      ... Early one morning Paul saw a spider crawling across the floor.

  Where? *Under the floorboards, out of a drawer, in the store cupboard, in the corner.*
      ... Early one morning Paul saw a spider crawling across the floor into the corner of the hall.

- These suggestions focus on /or/ words. Ask the children to choose some of the suggestions and write their own long sentence. They can then illustrate their spider's journey. Make a spider from black card and attach it to the page from a long length of black thread. They can then move it as they read out their sentence.

Variation

- Less able children could concentrate on the spelling of hall. Notice that when 'a' is followed by 'll' it is pronounced /or/.

  Make a list, including hall, wall, fall, etc.

  Children could write this out in alphabetical order.

Cross-curricular link

English: creative writing.

Underground

> Use old, damaged metal items to inspire your phonics teaching.

Suitable for

Children who are learning alternative graphemes.

Aims

To remind the children of the optional spellings of the phoneme /oi/.

Resources

- Some old metal items, including:
    a wire spring, or coiled-up wire
    aluminium foil
    a damaged metal toy (perhaps a car)
    an old pair of 'grandad' spectacles – broken in two
    a one-pound coin
- Optional: a large magnet, or even a metal detector, and a sand tray
- A prepared display board: brown paper suggesting soil, and a title, *'Leroy is using his metal detector. He finds …'* , and paper circles in the same brown paper (two per object)

What to do

- Tell the children about a little boy called Leroy who had a metal detector for his birthday. He went out into his garden to find treasure.
- Show the children the metal objects that Leroy found and help them to identify them all.
- Ask leading questions, e.g.
    - Do you think these spectacles were always like this?
    - Is this toy any use anymore?
    - What sort of coin is this?

- From these ideas you can then suggest phrases that describe the objects as they appear now, using as many /oi/ words as possible, e.g.
  - a pair of spectacles that used to be joined
  - a spoilt old toy
  - a piece of foil
  - a coiled-up piece of wire
  - a one-pound coin
- Remind the children of the two graphemes for /oi/ – 'oi' and 'oy', and notice where they are used in their phrases.
- Children work in pairs to produce pictures of Leroy's finds – one per paper circle. Fix these to the display.
- Cover each picture with a second brown paper circle on which you have written the object's description. Fix these in 'lift-the-flap' style.

Variation

- Hide the objects in a sand tray. Choose one child to use a large magnet to help Leroy find one of them. Take it in turns until all the objects are found and identified as above.

Cross-curricular link

Science: materials.

A winter's night

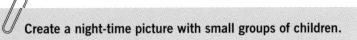

Create a night-time picture with small groups of children.

Suitable for

Children who are learning alternative graphemes.

Aims

To provide the children with examples of words containing the four graphemes for /ur/.

Resources

- A display board covered with dark-blue or purple paper
- Pieces of dark-coloured, or black, paper
- Scissors
- Four large sheets of paper labelled 'er', 'or', 'ir' and 'ur' to give to the children
- The following sentences (or ones of your own making) on individual cards:

  SET 1:

  Smoke is swirling up from the chimneys
  A bonfire is burning
  The curtains are closed in the third house along
  Ivy is curling up the old wall

  SET 2:

  Ferns are growing in the dirt between the stones
  An owl is perched in a tall fir tree with a worm in its beak
  A cat purrs as it licks its fur
  A person drops their purse
  People are returning home from work

What to do

- Repeat this basic activity with different groups using only one of the sets of sentences each time. Note: the artwork from Set 1 sentences needs to be on the display before the artwork from Set 2 can be added.
- Show the children the four labelled pieces of paper. Explain to them that these are different ways that they might need to spell the /ur/ sound. Read them out and spell them out loud with the children.
- Ask if anyone knows any word that would have one of these spellings. Write it down on the appropriate paper. Ask if anyone knows a word with a different spelling, write it down and then do the third and fourth options. Point out that after the letter 'w' the /ur/ phoneme is always spelt as 'or'.
- Divide the children into four groups and give one paper to each group. Tell them that they are going to collect words that have their spelling of the /ur/ sound.
- Explain to the children that you are going to read out some sentences about night-time. They should listen carefully for any words that have an /ur/ sound. There may be more than one word in some of the sentences.
- Now read out one of the sentences. Repeat it if necessary. Can the children tell you which of the words has the /ur/ sound in it? Does anyone think this word goes on their paper? Is it spelt with their grapheme? If so they should write it down. Continue in this way through all of your chosen sentences.
- Now ask one group to come to the front and show their paper. They should read each word in turn, allowing time for discussion. Was it on the right paper? Did anyone else write this one down? Who is right? Make any corrections.
- Divide the sentence cards between the children. They should work in pairs to cut out an outline shape from a dark paper to match their sentence, e.g. a cat, some people or an owl in a fir tree. These can be arranged on the display board with the sentences near them.

Variation

- This display can be used as a starting point for some writing. Using the sentences from your phonics work, they could think about ways to link them, or use any connectives they can to create a descriptive piece about night-time in the town.

Cross-curricular link

English: creative writing.

A spell for Josh

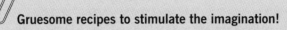

Gruesome recipes to stimulate the imagination!

Suitable for

Children who are learning alternative graphemes.

Aims

To help the children focus on the different ways that they might spell the phoneme /j/.

Resources

- Dictionaries
- A prepared display board: cover the board in a vivid colour. Cut out a large, black, sugar-paper pan and fix it to the display, with a wooden spoon sticking out of it. At the bottom right, attach a torn piece of paper – make it look scruffy – with the words, 'Stir it all up and just leave under a hedge for a jolly long time'.

What to do

- Explain to the children that today the witch (give her a long name beginning with the /j/ sound, making sure it's not someone in your class or school – perhaps Geraldine or Juliana) wants to create a new spell to make Josh jump so high that he can win the school sports day prize. Everything that goes into the spell must contain the sound /j/ somewhere in it.
- Encourage the children to come up with their own suggestions. Here are some to start you off:
  a giant's pyjamas
  a jumping gymnast
  a juicy jelly
  a gentle ghost
  a badger

> *a jaguar in a jacket*
> *a large lump of fudge*
> *a jar of jam*
> *a gigantic germ*
>
> - Explain to the children that they are going to write their chosen ingredient on a card, checking their spelling in the dictionaries.
> - Then they should cut it out 'with a jagged edge', before sticking it on the display. Place the cards as if they are being poured into the pan.

Variation

- Children could each write out a spell of their own. Collate these and make them into 'a book of spells for jumping gymnasts'.

Cross-curricular link

English: writing lists.

The playground

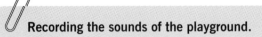

Recording the sounds of the playground.

Suitable for

Children who are learning alternative graphemes.

Aims

To create a visual and aural display of the /ee/ phoneme and some of its graphemes.

Resources

- Display board covered in blue paper at the top and green paper on the lower half
- Card and straws
- A few doll's house-sized figures of children
- A cassette recorder and blank cassette

What to do

- Explain to the children that they are going to create a display of a children's playground. It will have a slide and some swings. What else might they include?
- Help the children to make a slide. Use a long narrow strip of card (about 60cm x 4cm). Fold this along its length, and then snip along one side of the fold at 1cm intervals. Show the children how this allows the card to curve to make the shape of a slide. Attach it centrally to the display by stapling the slit edge to the board. Children can now add the slide's legs and ladder using the straws.
- Children can work in pairs to produce swings and other equipment from card and straws.
- Children can draw and cut out little figures and attach all the pieces to the display.

- Sit together as a group near the display. Use one of the dolls to show a child going down the slide. Make the sound 'wheeeeeee' yourself as you move it. Add plenty of intonation! What other sounds might they make? You want to encourage sounds that include the /ee/ phoneme, e.g. *shriek, scream, eek* – even *wheezing* and *weeping* if they have an accident.
- Choose a child to come out and move the doll, making a suitable sound word. What was this doll feeling? Frightened, scared, happy? How can they tell? Can the same sound word be interpreted in different ways by the tone of voice? Let the children experiment with this.
- Children can now record some of their sound words into the cassette recorder to make a collection of playground sounds – but all with an /ee/ in them.

Variation

- Cover the board with white paper and add some glitter. Make your slide from white card but without legs, ladder, etc. Add children in winter clothes for an icy day scene, when they are sliding on the ice. You can now add 'freezing' to your list of words.

Cross-curricular link

DT: shaping and assembling materials.

The Pharaoh's tomb

Who knows the secret of the tomb? Guess, then draw and add a label.

Suitable for

Children who are learning alternative graphemes.

Aims

To help the children remember when they need to use the 'mb' grapheme.

Resources

- Dictionaries

What to do

- Write the words 'In the catacombs of the tomb of the Pharaoh Ozyrumb' onto the whiteboard. Gather the children round the board and use a tone of voice to suggest sharing secret information.
- Tell the children that you have been exploring in Egypt and you were the first one to enter the tomb of the Pharaoh. Can the children read what is written on the board? That's where you went! Does anyone know what 'catacombs' are? (An underground burial place.)
- Tell them that inside the pyramid you found steps that led down into the catacombs. This is where the mummy of the Pharaoh Ozyrumb was placed.
- The strangest thing was that everything that had been placed in there with him matched the spelling of his name. Ask the children to look again at what you wrote on the board. Can they tell you the letters at the end of his name, and what is particular about them? 'It sounds like /m/ but it has a silent 'b' at the end.'

- Explain that you are now going to suggest some things that might – or might not – have been in there. Ask the children to put up their hand if they think it was in:
- Here are some ideas for you to name. Muddle the two lists as you go along.

  a statue of a **lamb**

  a bejewelled **comb**

  a **crumb** from some bread

  an unexploded **bomb**

  a **limb** broken from a golden statue

  a strange **thumb** print

  the stone from a **plum**

  a huge **drum** with a zig-zag pattern round it

  a baby's **pram**

  a **cream** cake

  a **dream** catcher made from feathers

  an old piece of chewing **gum**

  a picture of the Pharaoh's **mum**

  a toy **tram**

- The children are now going to record their ideas. They should write the title from the board and draw a large triangle to represent the pyramid. Inside the pyramid they should draw and label the things that were in the tomb – they should all end 'mb'. Outside the pyramid they should draw and label things that couldn't go in – they all end 'm'.
- Encourage them to use dictionaries to check their spellings.

Variation

- Able children might be able to write a story as if they were the explorer, describing what they saw and what was strange about it.

Cross-curricular link

History: customs and different ways of life.

Write a postcard

Make postcards and invent phrases using the /ear/ phoneme to write on them.

Suitable for

Children who are learning alternative graphemes.

Aims

To give children practice in writing words containing the phoneme /ear/.

Resources

- Plain postcards or pieces of white card cut to size

What to do

- Encourage the children to decorate their postcards with a colourful picture of the seaside or showing another holiday area or activity.
- Ask them to turn their card over and show them where to write their message on the left side of the reverse side of the postcard, leaving the right-hand side for the address.
- Help the children decide who they are sending the postcard to and explain they need to write *Dear* ... with their chosen name.
- Write the word *Dear* on the board and segment the word into its two phonemes – /d/ /ear/.
- Collect together suggestions of other words that have the phoneme /ear/ and list them on the board, e.g. *here, year, ear, cheer, pier, clear, appear*.
- Discuss the different spellings of the /ear/ phoneme.
  (If appropriate, also discuss homophones; i.e. words that sound the same but have different meanings for different spellings, e.g. *dear/ deer, peer/pier, hear/here*.

- Use the words in the list to create phrases that could be written on postcards.
  Ideas might include:
  Wish you were here
  Lovely to hear from you
  See you next year
  We have a clear view
  We walked down the pier
  Ring when you get near
  The sun will soon appear.
- Ask the children to write a short phrase containing the /ear/ phoneme on their postcard.
- Then sign them and write an address.
- Display the postcards by suspending them from the ceiling so they turn, thereby showing both the picture and the writing on the cards.

Variation

- Encourage the children to write their postcard to another child in the class, ensuring that everyone receives at least one card. Then post them into the class postbox. When you are sitting together in a circle, empty the contents of the postbox and ask each child to read aloud the message on their card.

Cross-curricular link

Geography: knowledge and understanding of places.

Out for a walk

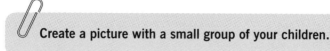

Create a picture with a small group of your children.

Suitable for

Children who are learning alternative graphemes.

Aims

To raise the children's awareness of the different ways that the phoneme /ow/ can be written.

Resources

- Art materials for sponging, cutting and sticking
- Felt-tip pens

What to do

- This is best done with a group of five or six children at a time.
- At the top of an A3 piece of paper put the title: 'Out for a walk'.
- Sponge-print a background of sky, hills, grass and a ploughed field (wavy lines).
- Cut out cloud shapes from white paper and large simple flower heads in a variety of colours, and stick them onto the background when it has dried.
  As the children do this, point out the words that have /ow/ in them: *ploughed, flower, clouds, brown, ground, out.*
- Children can now think of other objects or animals that have an /ow/ sound. Draw them, cut them out and add them to the picture. E.g. *cow, house, mouse, town, towel, power lines, tower.*

- Show the picture to the children and ask them to identify the main features you have put in.
  Write their suggestions onto the appropriate part of the picture:
      'clouds in the sky' – inside a cloud.
      'ploughed ground' – repeat the phrase all over the ground in the picture, following the wavy lines.
      'flowers all around' – write one word in each flower head.
- Discuss the different ways in which you have written the /ow/ sound.
- Children can now add words to their own drawings. Encourage them to check their spelling and think about the grapheme they need to use.

Variation

- Children can draw round their own shoe and cut it out. In each one write a word containing the /ou/ phoneme. Stick these on to create a route through your picture.

Cross-curricular link

Geography: places.

The Venus fly trap

A shared writing activity to solve the problem faced by the fly.

Suitable for

Children who are practising alternative graphemes.

Aims

To encourage the children to read, spell and write words with a variety of /igh/ graphemes.

Resources

- For the art activity:
  - Pictures of spiders and flies to copy
  - White paper, and strips of grey or cream paper for the window frame
  - A Venus fly trap plant
  - Glossy magazines
- For the writing activity:
  - A writing frame with the sections marked:
    Draw the problem and add labels
    The dangers
    A way out
  - Give it the title, *Fly, fly*
- For the variation activity:
  Brown, R. (1985) *The Big Sneeze*, *London*: Andersen Press Ltd

What to do

- Explain to the children that they are going to do some work about a spider and a fly. These two words share a common phoneme. Can anyone tell you what it is? (/igh/)
- Draw a spider-shaped mind map. Write the words *fly* and *spider* on the mind map and look carefully at the spellings. Can the children tell you any other words with this /igh/ phoneme? Add them to the mind map, e.g. *high, buy, sign, aisle, frightened, terrified, pile, sky.*

- To create their picture children should start by making a detailed drawing of a spider in the top corner of a sheet of white paper, and a fly slightly lower down. If they smudge the pencil lines using an eraser this can create an effect of movement or can be used to suggest a spider's web.
- Make a frame around this suggesting a window, keeping the colours pale.
- Look carefully at your Venus fly trap, then cut shapes from magazines to form the plant pot and the stems, leaves and flowers of the plant. Use magazines printed on high-quality paper to get the best effects.
- Glue the finished plant in the forefront of the window frame and add the spikes around the flowers with a metallic pen.
- Now, tell the children a story that involves a spider and a fly.

    One day the fly was crawling up a window pane. The spider had made a large web at the top of the window and the fly was getting very close to it. BUT there was another problem – on the windowsill itself there was a pot containing a very large Venus fly trap plant.

    How can the fly escape? Any higher and he might touch the web. Any lower and he might be eaten by the plant. What should he do to escape?

- Show the children the writing frame you have prepared. Read the headings for each section.
- The children should work as a group to identify the problem and suggest a solution to it.
- Challenge the children to use as many /igh/ words as they can in their work.

Variation

- Read the book *The Big Sneeze*, and enjoy the story and the illustrations. Go back through the book one page at a time listening out for words that contain the /igh/ phoneme. If you list them you should have: *by, fly, my, high, right, frightened, terrified, wife, spider*.

Cross-curricular link

Science: mini-beasts.

Chapter 8
Stage D

The guitar

Use this sound poem to show the ways in which endings may be added.

Suitable for

Children who are gaining confidence with spelling.

Aims

To practise doubling the consonant on one-syllable words before adding suffixes.

Resources

- Art material: three shades of A4 paper, scissors and glue
- A guitar that the children can handle
- Pictures of guitars in different styles – a music catalogue, or calendars with guitar photographs are available

What to do

- Draw the outline of a guitar onto a whiteboard or large sheet of paper before the lesson.
- Inside the shape, write out the following:

  Hip, hop, hum
  Tip, tap, strum
  Slip, slap, slam
  Jig, jag, jam
  Twang!

  Read this out with the children.
  Now ask them to imagine that this took place yesterday. How would it sound? Put the words into the past tense to find out. Do this orally at first.

- Can the children help you to write it down? Do the first line together.
  What spelling rule are they using? Who can explain it to the others?
  'One-syllable words ending vc (vowel, consonant) have the final consonant doubled before adding the 'ed' ending.'
- Ask the children to work independently on the poem until they reach the last word, *'Twang'*. Work with the children on this one. Encourage them to notice that there are already two consonants at the end of the word, which means that they don't need to double the final consonant before adding *'ed'*.
- Children can now make an image of a guitar of their own design. Fold one piece of paper in half lengthways and draw half a guitar body, and cut it out. Remember the hole for the sound.
  Cut a neck from the second shade of paper.
  Stick the third piece into their book or onto a backing paper, stick the body of the guitar on top and position the neck before sticking it down.
  Draw tuning pegs and frets with a pencil.
  Write the poem onto the picture in the past tense.

Variation

- Repeat the activity asking the children to change each word into its plural form.

Cross-curricular link

Science: sound.

Into the woods

> Use children's names for some interesting discussions about the oddities of our spelling.

Suitable for

Children who are gaining confidence with spelling.

Aims

To involve the children in spelling investigations.

Resources

- A display about a seasonal visit to the woods. E.g. for autumn, create trees by tearing brown sugar-paper trees and add texture to the trunk by adding vertical strips of different brown papers. Glue on several sheets of torn tissue paper in autumn shades to make the canopy of the leaves. Glue fallen leaves at the base of the display.
- Brown paper, tissue scraps and fine felt-tip pens

What to do

- Every child should make a small picture of a person to stick on the display of a class visit to the woods.
  Try: a torn piece of brown paper. Onto this stick an irregular, smaller piece of tissue paper. Onto this draw a picture of a person using a fine felt-tip pen.
- Explain to the children that they are going to work in pairs to name their two 'people'. They should choose two names that have the same phoneme. Look at these, notice the spelling and any variations in the graphemes.
- You will have to do some work on this as a group before you expect the children to do it independently. Start by asking the children to suggest any names that have the same phoneme somewhere in

them, or at the start, e.g. *Freddie, Freda*. Accept all suggestions, but move them on to notice that they could also have **Ph**oebe, **Fr**eddie. Here are some other ideas:

*Chris, **K**ylie*
***K**ate, **C**arol*
*Jameela, **Gi**llian*
***Th**omas, **T**racey*
George, James
*Nisha, **K**eith*
*Steven, Step**h**en*
*Grace, Te**ss***

- Stick the pictures of people onto your display in pairs as if they are walking through the woods. Make name labels and add them to the pictures.

Variation

- Challenge the children to find as many names beginning with the same phoneme (NOT letter, necessarily) as their own name.

Cross-curricular link

Science: seasons.

The stormy sea

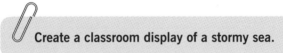

Create a classroom display of a stormy sea.

Suitable for

Children who are gaining confidence with spelling.

Aims

To provide a stimulus for exploring a range of graphemes that are pronounced /sh/.

Resources

- Tissue paper in shades of blue and green
- Brown sugar paper
- Plain backing paper and glue
- White paint and brushes

What to do

- Write this sentence on the board and read it to the children:

    The ferocious waves crashed onto the rocks, spraying their salty water like champagne across the ocean.

- Discuss any unfamiliar words with the children and encourage them to share their experiences of the sea. Has anyone seen waves crashing onto rocks? Do they think this sentence describes a calm or a stormy sea?
- Ask the children to help make a collage picture to illustrate this sentence.
- Cut the tissue paper into strips of varying lengths then glue them horizontally onto a plain, light backing paper, allowing them to overlap.

- Tear a few large, irregular-triangular shapes of slightly creased, brown sugar paper. Position these at intervals on the blue sea as rocks.
- Discuss how the sea would splash against the rocks and use thick white paint with a dry brush to create this effect of foam and spray.
- When your collage is complete, display the sentence across the base of the picture.
- Ask the children to look for the /sh/ phoneme in the text. Read the sentence aloud, asking them to put up their hand when they hear the /sh/ phoneme:

    fero-**ci**-ous
    cra-**sh**-ed
    ch-ampagne
    o-**ce**-an

Variations

- You might prefer to let the children use shades of blue and green paint to create the effect of waves. They could produce individual paintings and write the sentence themselves.
- More able children can segment the four words once they have identified the alternative /sh/ graphemes.

    Perhaps they'd like to tackle spelling other words that have the phoneme /sh/ spelt with these graphemes, e.g. *machine, Charlotte, quiche, precious, special* and *precocious*.

    NOTE: The spelling of *ocean* is an exception.

    How many different oceans can they name?

Cross-curricular link

Geography: physical features.

Fireworks

 Six activities based on your firework display.

Suitable for

Children who are gaining confidence with spelling.

Aims

To provide the children with opportunities to learn about and practise verb endings (suffixes).

Resources

- Create a firework display
- Add labels: cut out nine spiky shapes from brightly coloured card. Write one of your firework effect verbs on each one with a bold marker. Add glue and glitter to the edges. Pin these around your display.
- The following activities are based on these words: *fizz, whizz, bang, crash, flash, crackle, sparkle, shimmer, glitter*

What to do

Activity 1: **This is to help the children think about matching the endings of verbs to the past, present and future tenses.**

- Tell the children that they are going to create some sentences that start:

     Last year my fireworks …
     This year my fireworks are …
     Next year my fireworks will …

- Choose one of the words, e.g. *bang*.
- Explain to the children that to add this to the first sentence starter they will have to slightly change it. Ask for volunteers to say the sentence out loud and modify the word *bang*. It should become *banged*.

- Ask the children to spell this. Can they tell you what they did to the root word *bang* to change it into *banged*?
- Repeat this with each of the sentences in turn, making *banged, banging, bang*.
- Children can then try to do this with the root words *fizz, whizz, crash* and *flash*.

Activity 2: **This activity is a way to demonstrate the rules about dropping a final 'e' before adding 'ed' or 'ing'.**

- Put up the three words *shimmer, glitter* and *crackle* and ask the children to read them. Explain that you want to change *shimmer* to *shimmered*. Ask the children to tell you how to do it.
- Repeat with the word *glitter*, changing it to *glittered*.
- What about *crackle*? The children may respond with the same instruction – to add 'ed'. Do this and let them see the resulting word. Try reading it out loud. Can they spot the mistake? Ask the children to put the new instruction into words – it needs to be: *Take off the 'e' before adding 'ed'*.
- Work the same way as you devise the rules for the suffix 'ing'.
- The children can now write out these words – one per card. Use as many of the nine root words as necessary to have one card per child in your class. The nine words will give a total of 27 cards. Collect them in and check the spellings before using them for the next activity.

Activity 3: **This is a short game to practise reading the words.**

- Distribute the cards made in Activity 2 so that everyone has one. Tell the children that you are going to say a sentence containing one of the words on the cards. If the child has that word they should raise their card. Use sentences based on the format, e.g.
  - Last year my firework glittered.
  - This year my firework will whizz.
  - Next year I hope my firework will shimmer.
- Do this in a quick way so that the children don't get bored. Repeat some of the words to keep them listening.

Activity 4: **A spelling game.**

- Before the activity, cut out nine spiky shapes. On each one write the letters that make up one of the words from your firework display. Muddle the letters up and scatter them over the spiky shape. If the cards on the display are on coloured card make sure you use different colours for these muddled versions.

- The children sit with you in a small group, near the display.
- Show them one of the muddled words. Who can work out which firework word the letters could spell? They can take the card and go to the display and hold it near the correct spelling. If they get it right they can choose the next muddled word to hold up.
- Cards could be replaced in the pile to allow everyone to have a go.

Activity 5: **An active game that needs a lot of space and some music.**

- Children stand in a space, each holding one of the word cards from Activity 2.
- Explain to them that when the music plays they are to move around the room and every time they meet another child they should swap their word cards.
- When the music stops they have to find the other two children with the same root words, e.g. *crackle* will be looking for *crackled* and *crackling*. When they are together they should sit down in the following order – last year, this year and then next year.
- When all the children are ready, choose one set and ask them to say what is on the cards, in that same order, e.g.

  Last year my firework crackled.
  This year my firework is crackling.
  Next year my firework will crackle.

- Then put the music on and start the game again.

Activity 6: **Writing poems based on these words.**

- Tell the children that they are going to create their own firework poem using some of the words from your firework display. Share some of these ideas with the children first, or write one together.
- The finished poems could be collated into an anthology of firework poems. Use a Word program on the computer for the text. Add illustrations later, or print them onto brightly coloured paper. Some ideas:

    My fireworks
    Crackled, shimmered and glittered
    Last year

    My fireworks are
    Crackling, shimmering and glittering
    This year
    Etc.

    My fireworks whizzed and fizzed last year
    My fireworks are whizzing and fizzing this year
    What do you think they'll do next year?
    Will they whizz and fizz?

    Sparkling and crackling
    Shimmering and glittering
    Went my fireworks last year
    Etc.

Cross-curricular link

History: Guy Fawkes and bonfire night.

A counting book

Practise your phonics as you make a book for a younger child.

Suitable for

Children who are gaining confidence with spelling.

Aims

To make counting books for younger children with a phonic theme, as children test out their knowledge.

Resources

- Prepare books, one for each child, from three sheets of A4 paper, folded in half and stapled

What to do

- Explain to the children that they are going to make a counting book to hand to a child in the Early Years class. Give the books out and ask the children to write their name very lightly on the first page, as this will become the cover and they may want to put it in a different place when they plan their cover design.
- They should now go through the first 10 pages of the book putting the numbers 1 to 10 in the top corner of each page. Again, they should write lightly so that they can change the numbers it to a more interesting form later.
- Ask everyone to find the page marked '5'. On this page they are going to write the words 'five fat elephants'.
- Before they do this, ask them, 'What is special about this phrase?'. Will they spot the one phoneme /f/ that is in each word? They might also be able to tell you that it is spelt in different ways. Ask for volunteers to come out and write the phrase on the board.

- Repeat this with the phrase for page number '8'. This is a tricky one for children to create. We suggest: 'eight electric engines'.
- The children can now complete these two pages in their own books. Remind them that they should check their spellings before writing them onto the page, as it is important that the younger children see it spelt correctly. They can then illustrate these two pages.
- Children can complete their number books independently, before adding a cover design.
- Children can be as creative as possible but here are some suggested phrases for the other numbers in case they need help;
    one wonderful wizard
    two terrible tigers
    three thin things
    four funny frogs
    six silly seats
    seven sneezing centipedes
    nine naughty gnomes
    ten tall trees

Variation

- More able children could be given a more limited challenge so that they don't take the first idea that they have. They could make it counting animals.

Cross-curricular link

Maths: counting.

The case of the missing letter

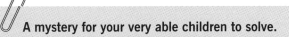

A mystery for your very able children to solve.

Suitable for

Children who are gaining confidence with spelling.

Aims

To challenge able children to think about the oddities of some of the letters in the English language – especially 'w' – BUT don't tell the children!

Resources

- A copy of a comic-strip story, entitled: *DI Squirt and The Missing Letter*. The layout for the story consists of seven frames, into six of which the children will be adding illustrations, with speech bubbles, etc., as in a comic strip. There are captions for each of the frames for the children to read:

  Frame 1: a blank rectangular frame. Caption: *An old lady came to Detective Inspector Squirt one day and said that one of the letters that had been stuck on her fridge had gone missing.*

  Frame 2: a blank rectangular frame. Caption: *She thought a squirrel that she'd once seen acting strangely in her garden might have it.*

  Frame 3: a cloud shape in which are written the words: *DI Squirt set off on a quest, following the trail that the squirrel had left.*

  Frame 4: a blank rectangular frame. Caption: *He squelched through the mud.*

  Frame 5: a blank rectangular frame. Caption: *He squeezed through the fence after his quarry.*

  Frame 6: a blank rectangular frame. Caption: *He quaked in his boots, then ...*

  Frame 7: a larger blank rectangular frame. Caption: *... he saw, over the field, a whole load of the creatures, each carrying two swords!*

What to do

- Sit round a table so that everyone in the group can see the copy of the story.
- Tell them that this is a detective mystery for them to solve. Read the captions to tell the story, with the children helping you.
- Explain to the children that their task is to discover what the missing letter is. Tell them that the clues are in the words of the story, so they should read it very carefully. Allow time for them to think about it and discuss with each other any ideas that occur to them.
- If they need a clue, wait a few minutes before telling them: 'Now you can hear it – but it can't be seen. Then it appears when it hasn't been spoken.'
- When they solve it or you consider that they have taken their investigation as far as they can, ask them to share their ideas with you. If necessary, explain it to them:

  In the first six frames of the story, they will hear the sound /w/ – but there is no letter 'w' anywhere in those captions.
  In the last frame they will see several letter 'w's but they cannot hear them at all.
  So, the missing letter is **'W'**.

- Children can now illustrate their story, adding speech bubbles or sound-effect words.

Variation

- Children can complete the story. Does DI Squirt apprehend the culprits and get the letter back for the old lady?

Cross·curricular link

English: story writing.

Celebration at the space station

Inter-planetary spelling for a group of up to 12 children.

Suitable for

Children who are gaining confidence with spelling.

Aims

To focus on the word-ending 'tion' and its many graphemes.

Resources

- A large copy of the poem, with the last word (the rhyming words) on each line left off:

    What an (occasion!)
    They came to the (station)
    From many a (nation)

    Filled with (elation)
    The boy and the (Martian)
    Crossed over the starry (ocean)

    They joined the (procession)
    Admired all the (fashion)
    And purchased a magical (potion)

    A trip to the (station)
    Oh! What a (sensation)
    For the boy and his friend, Marty (Martian)

- Strips of paper and removable adhesive (these will be added to the ends of the lines of the poem eventually)
- Dictionaries
- For the variation: marbled paper (made some days before so that it is dry), felt-tip pens and glitter glue

What to do

- Read the poem to the children without them seeing it. Ask them if they notice anything. Did they spot the rhymes? All of the lines of the poem end with the same rhyme.
- Now show them your copy of the poem with the missing rhymes. Read it again. The children may like to join in. Don't forget to say the missing words.
- Tell the children that they are to write out the missing words. Give each child a strip of paper and explain that you will read it to them again and as you say each missing word you will point to one child. That child has to go off quietly and use the dictionaries or write that one word from memory. They should write it large enough to be read from the board. They should rejoin you as soon as they have written it. Some of the words are repeated, but they should still be given out as they occur in the poem.
- Now read the poem again, pointing to the children as you go along.
- When all the children have rejoined the group you read it once more, letting the children come out as their word is said so they can stick their strip of paper in place.
- How many variations of 'tion' are there?
  ('tion', 'tian', 'sion', 'ssion', 'shion'.)

Variation

- Children could create a space scene from their marbled paper – both for the background, and for cutting out into the shapes of planets and spacecraft. Add details with felt-tip pens and then use glitter to add some magic.

Cross-curricular link

Science: forces.

Make a bridge

Set the children a challenge using adjectives ending with 'er' and 'est'.

Suitable for

Children who are gaining confidence with spelling.

Aims

To develop children's interest in using adjectives with the suffixes 'er' and 'est'.

Resources

- Junk materials
- Tape, scissors and glue
- Card and pens for labelling
- Parcel labels for badges

What to do

- Set the children a challenge to build a bridge using junk materials. It may be appropriate for the children to work in pairs.
- Tell them that when everyone has completed the task the class is going to vote for the best bridge in each category.
  (Decide whether to choose the categories before or after the children make their bridges.)
- Discuss together what the categories will be, e.g. *long, tall, wide, narrow, low, short, strong, neat.*
- Write the words on the board, encouraging the children to spell the words as you write.
- Introduce the comparative and superlative terms, e.g. *long, longer, longest; tall, taller, tallest.*
  Add these words to the list you have already written up, noting the suffixes 'er' and 'est'.

- When the children have completed their bridge designs, measure and test the models and decide who are the winners.
- Let the children create labels that can stand up alongside the finished bridges by folding pieces of card. Write on them, e.g.
  A long bridge.
  A longer bridge (you might need several of these).
  The longest bridge.
- Help the children write on plain parcel stickers to create badges that they can wear, e.g.
  I made the longest bridge.
  My bridge was longer than Sam's bridge.

Variation

- Rather than using junk materials you could ask the children to make bridges using plasticine or modelling clay.

Cross-curricular link

DT: evaluating products.

Poppies

Use this beautiful painting to inspire paintings of huge red poppies, then focus on the other plurals that follow this spelling pattern.

Suitable for

Children who are gaining confidence in spelling.

Aims

To encourage children to practise the plural spelling of words ending with 'y'.

Resources

- A copy of *Poppies* by Georgia O'Keeffe
- Paints, brushes and paper
- A5 pieces of paper folded horizontally

What to do

- Look at a reproduction of this painting.
- Enjoy painting some huge red poppies that fill the paper.
- Tell the children if they have painted two or more flowers they need to write *Poppies* as the title of their picture.
- Then ask them what they should write if they had only painted one poppy.
  Can anyone spell *poppy*?
- Remind the children that words ending with the letter 'y' can't be made plural by simply adding 's'. Can anyone remember the rule?
  Change the 'y' to 'i' and add 'es'.
- Ask the children for suggestions of other words that follow this pattern and write these on the board, e.g. *baby, penny, lady, baddy, goody, cherry, city, party, berry, fly, story.*

- Give the children the folded pieces of paper and ask them to write one of the words on each piece.
- The children can then open the fold to write the plural inside. The papers can then be displayed around their paintings.
- Or, if you prefer an interactive display, the papers can be left blank inside before pinning them on a display board so the children can open them and add the plural version of the word later.

Variation

- More able children can be challenged to find other words that have 'es' rather than 's' for plurals – *all those ending in 'ss', 'ch', 'sh' or 'zz', e.g. cross, lunch, brush, buzz.*

Cross-curricular link

Art: investigating work by different artists.

Part 3
Exploring sounds

Chapter 9
Stage A

Yummy yoghurts

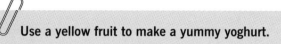
Use a yellow fruit to make a yummy yoghurt.

Suitable for

Children who are practising single-letter phonemes.

Aims

To help children use and remember the phoneme /y/.

Resources

- Natural yoghurt
- Lemons
- Bananas
- Sugar
- Bowls and spoons

What to do

- Tell the children that they are going to make a new yoghurt.
- Explain that you are going to add fruit to a natural yoghurt to make it yummy but that these are special yoghurts that only have yellow fruit in them.
- Ask them which fruits are yellow. Then show them the lemon and the banana and let them choose which they'd like to use to make their yoghurt yummy.
- Demonstrate how to squeeze the juice from the lemon and peel and chop the banana.
- As the children prepare their chosen fruit and add it to the yoghurt, encourage them to repeat the phrase *yummy yellow yoghurt* and point out how many /y/ phonemes they are using.
- Taste the yoghurt and decide if it needs more sugar to make it yummy.

- Ask if they are happy with the taste and when they answer 'Yes', does anyone notice this is another word beginning with /y/?
- Perhaps the children could report on the activity the next day, then they can talk about the **y**ummy **y**oghurts they made **y**esterday!

Variation

- Other food-related ideas to make could be Juicy jellies or Krispie cakes.

Cross-curricular link

DT: food.

The teacher's pet

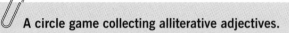 A circle game collecting alliterative adjectives.

Suitable for

Children who are practising single-letter sounds.

Aims

To encourage children to identify and remember a range of initial phonemes.

What to do

- Sit in a circle and tell the children that you have got a new pet dog.
- Explain to the children that you are going to think of an adjective to describe your pet – 'energetic'.
  Does anyone know what that means? He's lively and has got lots of energy. He's always ready to go for a run.
  (Use this opportunity to extend the children's vocabulary.)

  The teacher's dog is an energetic dog.

  Does anyone know what sound 'energetic' begins with?
  Write the phoneme /e/ on the board.
- Ask the children to think of other ways to describe a dog that begin with this sound. Suggestions might include:
  excellent, educated, elegant, excited, edgy, eleven, empty, endangered, extra (this word allows any descriptive word to be used, e.g. extra small).
- Now tell the children they are going to use words that begin with this sound as you play the game. Explain that the first person describes the teacher's pet then the next person must repeat the start of the sentence and think of another word beginning with the same sound to describe the pet, and so on round the circle.

- For example, you can begin by saying:

  The teacher's pet is an energetic dog.

  Then the second person might say:

  The teacher's pet is an excited dog.

  Then the third person continues:

  The teacher's pet is an excellent dog.

- Continue around the circle until everyone has had a turn. Tell the children it's okay to repeat words. It can be lots of fun if the children start to use less appropriate adjectives, e.g. elastic, elbow, eggy.
- Count up how many different adjectives you thought of beginning with /e/ and write the number underneath the phoneme on the board.
- Then start the game off again with a different initial phoneme.
- 'Now I'm going to think of an adjective to describe my pet that begins with /d/.

  The teacher's pet is a delightful dog.

  Can anyone think of another word to describe my dog beginning with this sound?

  Let's see how many adjectives we can think of that begin with /d/.'
  Write this phoneme on the board.

- Continue the game around the circle until everyone has had a turn. Praise the children who use a new word or remember an unusual adjective from a previous game.
- When you play the game again you may decide to repeat the same initial phonemes if the children need more practice, or try some new ones.

Variation

- You could play the game with a different teacher's pet each time and choose adjectives that start with the same initial phoneme as the pet.
  Here are some ideas: *dangerous dog, cute cat, restless rabbit, heavy horse, slippery snake,* or *an enormous elephant!*

Cross-curricular link

English: extending children's vocabulary of adjectives.

Simon says ...

A different version of a familiar game, focusing on a range of initial sounds.

Suitable for

Children who are practising single-letter sounds.

Aims

To encourage children to use their auditory discrimination skills to identify the odd one out when listening to a range of initial phonemes.

What to do

- Take the children into a large space and have them all facing you.
- Tell them about the game. It's a different version of Simon says ... Explain that Simon is going to tell them to do various actions that all begin with the same phoneme. Today's phoneme is /w/.
- Warn the children that they must listen carefully and not be caught out, because sometimes you will be slipping in an instruction that doesn't begin with that sound.
  And if they do that action they will be out!
- Have a practice turn.
  Demonstrate the actions each time for the children to copy:
  Simon says ... wave.
  Simon says ... walk.
  Simon says ... wink.
  Simon says ... wiggle.
  Simon says ... jump.
- Who jumped with you? Who did you catch out?
- Play the game with a range of active verbs.
  Suggestions include:
  smile, stand up straight, stride, stretch, sit.
  Or *hop, hands on head, hug, hoot, hunch, hum.*

Variation

- It's great fun thinking up actions for these verbs – perhaps you could set the children a challenge to think of as many as they can for all the phonemes they know. Keep a list of them and practise them at spare moments – *Show me an action that begins with 'g'.*
  E.g. *gallop, glare, giggle, gaze, groan, gulp, gasp.*

Cross-curricular link

English: using verbs.

Guesssss

A guessing game that only has clues beginning with sssssssssssss.

Suitable for

Children who are practising single-letter sounds.

Aims

To help the children recognise and use the phoneme /s/.

What to do

- Tell the children you are going to play a special guessing game.
- Explain that they must listen very carefully to the clues.
  'Can you *guessss* something sticky?'
- Choose a child to answer – *anything sticky is correct*.
- Then give another clue:
  'Can you guessss something small?'
  Let another child answer before giving a third clue:
  'Can you guessss something slow?'
- When the third clue has been answered, ask the children if they have noticed anything about these sssspecial clues.
- Does anyone think they can give a sssspecial clue?
  Have the children worked out the rule?
  The clue has got to be something beginning with **/s/**.
- Once the children understand the rule they can take turns.
  When someone answers a clue correctly they have the chance to say a new clue.
  There are lots of adjectives beginning with /s/. Try: *salty, sad, safe, sandy, secret, slimy, sparkling, steamy, sudden, sweet.*

Variation

- You might like to suggest the children play this game at home with their parents and carers. Maybe you can make a collection of adjectives beginning with /s/. We thought of over 70. Challenge the children and adults to see how many they can find. There will be many unfamiliar words for the children, e.g. *slender*, *snarling*, *severe*, so this provides an opportunity to extend their vocabulary.

Cross-curricular link

English: using adjectives.

Listen before you leap

> The ladybird leaps if it can land on a place beginning with /l/.

Suitable for

Children who are practising single-letter sounds.

Aims

To help children hear and use the phoneme /l/.

What to do

- Tell the children that in this game the ladybird can only land on places beginning with the sound /l/.
- Sit in a class circle and choose one child to go into the middle. That child crouches down to become the ladybird.
  To start the game the teacher says:

  The ladybird landed on a …

  Ask the children sitting in the circle to put up their hand if they want to make a suggestion.
- The ladybird in the middle points to a child to say a word.
  If the word begins with /l/, all the class repeat the sentence and the ladybird leaps over and exchanges places with the child who made the suggestion. The child who said the word then becomes the ladybird.
  If the word suggested does not begin with /l/, the child in the centre remains the ladybird and chooses another child to complete the sentence and the game continues.
  Suitable nouns beginning with /l/: *ladder, lamb, lamp, lap, lantern, lawn, lead, leg, lemon, leopard, letter, lettuce, lollipop.*

Variation

- Write out the start of the sentence on pieces of card and allow the children to choose the ending from a range of pictures. They must find something that begins with /l/.

Cross-curricular link

Science: mini beasts.

Spot the odd one out

An opportunity for children to discriminate between initial phonemes.

Suitable for

Children who are practising single-letter sounds.

Aims

To help children to listen carefully and identify phonemes.

What to do

- Tell the children that you are going to play a special listening game.
- Explain that you are going to say three words and they must pick the odd one out. Ask the children to listen carefully and to raise their hand if they know the odd one.
- Start with fruits: *avocado – apple – banana*.
  Listen to the children's ideas.
  Some children might find this activity quite difficult as you are asking them to focus on the sound rather than the meaning of the words. But it's interesting to see if anyone can spot it!
- Explain to the children that two of the words begin with the same initial sound /a/ but one of them does not, so that is the odd one out.
- Try another three words: *television – computer – telephone*.
- Then three more: *Simon – Edward – Stephen*.
- If the children are struggling to grasp the concept ask them to help you think of three words with an odd one out using these suggestions:
    Food: jelly – jam – ...
    Colours: blue – brown – ...
    Animals: tiger – tortoise – ...
    Vehicles: bike – bus – ...
    Play equipment: slide – swings – ...

Variation

- You can play an easier version of the game by listing any three unrelated things with two sharing the same initial sound.

Cross-curricular link

Science: sorting, naming and describing things.

Jim went to the gym

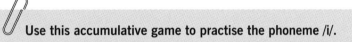

Use this accumulative game to practise the phoneme /i/.

Suitable for

Children who are practising single-letter sounds.

Aims

To encourage children to hear and use the phoneme /i/.

Resources

- A sports bag

What to do

- Tell the children that you are going to play a remembering game.
- Show them the sports bag and tell them this is Jim's bag, and that Jim has got his gym things in his bag because he's going to the gym. Don't write the title down unless you want to teach the children about alternative graphemes for the phoneme /i/.
- Explain that everything in his bag doesn't need to be used at the gym but they must have the /i/ sound in them – like J**i**m and g**y**m.
- If it's the first time you are playing this game you might need to spend some time thinking of suitable words, e.g. *whistle, bin, chips, fiddle, crisps, whisky, chicken, pretty wings, zipped jacket, little engine, big fish, plastic pig.*
- To make the game easier, tell the children they can use *little … plastic … big …* and *pretty …* in front of any other word:
  - *a plastic bottle*
  - *a big towel*
  - *a little book*
  - *a pretty cup.*

- Sit in a circle and start the game by saying:

  When Jim went to the gym he had his gym shoes in his bag.

- The child next to you in the circle repeats:

  When Jim went to the gym he had his gym shoes ...

  (then adds another item) *... and a whistle in his bag.*

- The child next to them repeats the sentence with the whistle and adds another item to go in his bag:

  When Jim went to the gym he had his gym shoes, a whistle ... and a pin in his bag.

- Continue around the circle adding items into the bag. How many can you remember?

Variation

- You could play this game with initial phonemes by changing the title:

  When Melissa went to market ...
  When Daniel went to the doctor ...
  When Holly went on holiday ...

Cross-curricular link

PSHE: keeping fit.

Rainbow games

A set of four activities to practise spelling and reading simple CVC words.

Suitable for

Children who are practising single-letter sounds.

Aims

To practise alphabetical order, and to make and read CVC words.

Resources

- Print and laminate sets of cards for the 26 individual letters of the alphabet; make them business-card size
  Use a different-colour font for each set **or** print each set onto a different colour of card or paper

What to do

Activity 1: **Make a rainbow, sequencing the letters of the alphabet.**

- The children should sit two to a table using two different-coloured packs of alphabet cards.
- Each child arranges their pack of cards in alphabetical order. They should make a rainbow arch by laying 'a' at the bottom left of their table , 'z' at the bottom right of their table and 'm' at the top centre of their table. They can now fill in the gaps by placing the rest of the cards.

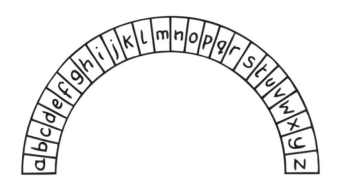

- Ask each child to read their cards out loud to check that they have them in the right order.
- Ask the children to identify their five vowel cards. Now they should swap their set of vowels with the other child at their table, and place the new vowel cards into their rainbow arch. Because they are in different colours this makes the vowels and consonants clearly observable.

Activity 2: **Children use a hands-on approach to create and change words.**

- Lay out your alphabet arches as before, with two children at a table. Ask the children to swap their vowel letter cards.
- Explain to the children that they are going to make the word *cat*. Ask the children to choose the initial sound (consonant) and place it in the space in the middle of their rainbow. They then choose the vowel and place that to the right of the first card, and then the final consonant to complete the word. Read the word 'cat' together.
- Ask the children to remove the 'c' and replace it in the right place in their rainbow. Now find 's' and put that at the start of your word. What does it say now?
- Continue in this way, changing one letter at a time to make new words.

Activity 3: **Reading rainbows. This time the children have to work out the spelling.**

- Now play again, telling the children to find the letters to make 'pot'. Say the word clearly, stressing the three separate phonemes. Check to see that everyone has the correct spelling before moving on.
- Ask the children to listen carefully as you tell them the next word. Remind them that they will only have to change one of the letters.
- Can they turn 'pot' into 'hot', for example? Watch to see who can find the necessary letter and position it correctly.
- Continue in this way, for as long as interest is maintained.

Activity 4: **Share a rainbow. Spell and read your words with friends.**

- Play either of the first two games as a small group activity with those who need some additional practice.
- Sit near a whiteboard. Using removable adhesive, position the cards in a rainbow arch as before onto the whiteboard. Do this as a group exercise asking for help, suggestions, volunteers, etc. This is useful as an activity in its own right for those who are struggling.
- Ask one child to come out and make the given word, e.g. peg. Does everyone agree that it is right?
- Choose another child to come out and take away the letter 'p'. Now put a letter 'l' in its place. Who can read this new word?
- Continue round the group.

Variation

- Leave a completed rainbow arch on a whiteboard or wall near your class word-bank. Encourage the children to use it for checking their spelling.

Cross·curricular link

English: interacting in groups.

Real or nonsense words

Children work in groups of three to play this game to make and read words and non-words.

Suitable for

Children who are practising single-letter sounds.

Aims

To provide an opportunity for children to read random three-letter CVC words.

Resources

- For each set of three children:
  - Two sets of alphabet cards from the Rainbow activities (see pages 234–7)
  - Two sheets of A4 paper labelled *Real words* and *Nonsense words*

What to do

- Separate the alphabet cards into consonants and vowels.
- With the children in groups of three, hand out the packs of cards:
  Child One has a consonant pack
  Child Two has vowels (give them both sets)
  Child Three has consonants.
  They should sit at the table in the order: consonant, vowel, consonant.
- Ask the children to shuffle their cards without looking at the letters on them, and keep them face down.
- In turn, each child places their top card on the table and reads it out loud. Keep the order as set.
- Can they now read the word they have made? Is it a real word? Or a nonsense word?
  They should record it on the appropriate paper.

- Place the cards back in their packs, and shuffle them again before making another word.
- They should continue until they have at least five words on each sheet of paper.
- When you want to check their work, do it by asking the children to read out the words they have made.

Variation

- This game can be played with three dice. Use three wooden cubes in different colours and write some letters on them: consonants on two of them and vowels on the third. Children can work individually, each with a set of dice, to make and record real and nonsense words as before.

Cross-curricular link

English: interacting in groups.

Two for one

> Keep the letters in the same order but move your position to read a new word.

Suitable for

Children who are practising single-letter sounds.

Aims

To give the children practice in oral blending.

Resources

- Five pieces of A4 card with one large letter on each – *p, e, t, n, i* for:
  ten and *net*
  pin and *nip*

What to do

- Gather a group of six or more children together.
- Practise the sound for each phoneme you are using today.
- Stand the first three cards up on display so the children can use their oral blending skills to find the word, e.g. *ten*.
- Repeat with *pin*.
- Take the children outside or into a large space.
- Choose three children to hold a card. Position them in a vertical line down the centre of the room with the 'e' between the 't' and the 'n'. Make sure everyone has their letter the correct way up!
- Take the rest of the children to the left-hand side of the room and ask the children holding the cards to turn towards you and show their cards.
  What does the word say?
  Point to the first letter on the left and help the children decode the word t-e-n – *ten*.

- Take the children to the right-hand side of the room and ask the children holding the cards to turn towards you and show their cards. What does the word say now? Look carefully.
  Point to the first letter on the left and help the children decode the word n-e-t – *net.*
  It's changed!
  Can the children explain why we can read two different words when we move across the room?
- Collect the children together and try again with a different set of letters to read p-i-n and n-i-p.

Variation

- With more able children you might like to try four-letter words.
  Use the letters s, t, o, p, a, r to make *stop* and *pots; star* and *rats.*
  Can you think of any other words that can be read either way?

Cross-curricular link

English: wordplay.

Do you know?

Children can increase their general knowledge as they practise their initial sounds.

Suitable for

Children who are practising single-letter sounds.

Aims

To help the children concentrate on initial letter sounds as they test, and improve, their general knowledge.

Resources

- A set of letters on individual cards in a container; choose ones that your children are currently focusing on
- Three labels: 'animals', 'colours', 'names'

What to do

- This activity is best done with a small group of children.
- Place the three labels where the children can easily see them. Read them together, making sure the children know what they say.
- Choose one child to reach into the container and pick out a letter card. Can they tell you what letter it is? What sound does it make?
- Explain to the group that you want them to think of any animal beginning with that sound. Accept as many ideas as the children can think of. Next they will think of a colour beginning with that sound, and then a name, e.g. the letter *w* is chosen and the children suggest *whale, white, William*.
- Repeat the game with a letter picked out by each child in the group in turn.
- This should be an oral activity as their word choices are based on sound not spelling.

Variations

- Change the categories each time you play it, but keep them quite broad to make the game accessible for young children.
- A more complicated version for more able children is on page 302

Cross-curricular link

Science: animals and colours.

Chapter 10
Stage B

Whoosh! Crash!

An active circle game for all the class, using two words that end with the same sound.

Suitable for

Children who are learning graphemes with more than one letter.

Aims

To help children remember and practise the phoneme /sh/.

Resources

- A large space

What to do

- The children all stand in a circle with an adult or teacher.
- Explain to the children that you are going to play a game using the words 'whoosh' and 'crash'. They are onomatopoeic words so ask for ideas of when you might use these words to describe sounds, e.g. a rocket firework shooting in the sky or Humpty Dumpty falling off a wall.
- Demonstrate the action for 'whoosh' by holding out your arms in front, to the right, then sweeping them across to your left side. Let the children practise this movement as they say 'whoosh'.
- Now show them how to pass the 'whoosh' around the circle with one person at a time moving their arms and saying 'whoosh'. You start the action then the next child on your left repeats the action – sending the 'whoosh' from one child to the next all around the circle. Practise passing the 'whoosh' around the circle in this way.

- Once the children have mastered the 'whoosh' movement in one direction, explain that at some point you are going to clap your hands and shout 'crash'. When they hear this 'crash' they must reverse the direction of the 'whoosh' so that it passes from the left to the right.
- Continue playing the game in this way by changing the direction occasionally but unexpectedly to increase the fun!

Variation

- When the children are competent and confident with the game you can elect two children to make the crash sound when they choose.

Cross-curricular link

English: developing vocabulary.

Something and nothing

The children try to keep an object hidden as it's passed around the circle. Guess who has it? Keep a tally of the guesses – did they have *something* or *nothing*?

Suitable for

Children who are learning graphemes of more than one letter.

Aims

To provide children with an opportunity to practise reading two words containing the phoneme /th/.

Resources

- Small object such as a plastic cube

What to do

- Write the two words up on a board at the front of the group:
  Something   Nothing
  'What do you notice about these two words?'
  They are compound words with two different prefixes added to the word *thing*.
- Ask the children to sit in a circle and show them the cube or small object that they are going to pass around. Tell them they must try really hard to keep the object hidden, so they should pass the object from one to another behind their backs. Let the children try this.
- Now explain that you are going to try to spot who has the object as they pass it round the circle. Give the object to a child and encourage the children to continue passing the object as you count slowly up to 10. Then try to guess who has it.

- If you guess correctly the child shows the object and says 'something' and can put a tally mark under the word **something**. If you guess wrongly and they open both hands to show they have 'nothing', the child can put a tally mark under the word **nothing**.
- Ask the children to choose a number beginning with the phoneme /th/. This will be the target number – when one of the tally lists reaches this number the game is over. Try 3 and 13 but avoid 30 or a 1000 or you'll be there until bedtime!
- Now choose a child to be in the middle of the circle. Ask them to close their eyes as the children start to move the object round the circle, then count up to 10 before the object stops and they must guess who is holding the object behind their back.
- If they guess correctly they can have another go, but if they are wrong they must exchange places with the child who has the object. This child then goes into the middle and the game starts again.
- Play until your tallying reaches the target number under one of the words.

Variation

- You can play the game by collecting cubes in a tub. Label two tubs 'something' and 'nothing'. Decide whether to use three or thirteen cubes and lay them out in the centre of the circle. Use one of the cubes to play the game and when it is spotted it is put into the tub marked 'something'. Continue playing until the cubes are all collected in the tub labelled 'something'.

Cross-curricular link

Mathematics: tallying.

Strong string

Make a new word by changing one letter at a time.

Suitable for

Children who are learning graphemes of more than one letter.

Aims

To encourage children to enjoy wordplay and practise spelling words with the phoneme /ng/.

Resources

- Whiteboard or magnetic letters

What to do

- Ask the children to segment the word **strong** into its five phonemes: s-t-r-o-ng.
- Write the word on the board or make it using the magnetic letters. Space the letters out into their phonemes.
- Show the children how to change the 'o' to make a new word: s-t-r-i-ng.
- Encourage the children to use oral blending to read the new word.
- Now suggest taking away the 'r' to make a new word: s-t-i-ng.
- Who can use their oral blending skills to read the new word?
- Challenge the children to remove another letter and create a different word.
- Carry on like this, altering a letter at a time:
    s – i -ng
    s – a – ng
    b -a -ng
    r -a -ng
- Can you get back to **strong** or **string**?

Variation

- You might set a challenge for the children to work in pairs to see who can make the longest list. If they record their work they can explain the process to the other children.

Cross-curricular link

Science: forces.

Warm up with phonics

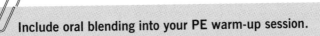

Include oral blending into your PE warm-up session.

Suitable for

Children who are learning graphemes with more than one letter.

Aims

To give the children an opportunity for oral blending.

What to do

- Take the children into an open space and ask them to spread themselves out so they are each in a space of their own.
  Stand at the front of the group.
- Explain that you are going to segment the names of PE equipment into all the separate sounds or phonemes.
  The children must repeat each phoneme after you and try to work out the word.
  Which piece of equipment is it?
- Clap your hands above your head after you say:
  'Give me a /b/'.
  The children repeat the /b/ and copy the clap.
- Clap your hands to one side after you say:
  'Give me an /or/'.
  The children repeat the /or/ and copy the clap.
- Clap your hands to the other side after you say:
  'Give me a /l/'.
  The children repeat the /l/ and copy the clap.

- Finally, ask – 'What have you got?'.
  The children can shout back: 'ball!'.
  Here is a list of PE equipment segmented into phonemes:
    b-ea-n b-a-g
    h-oo-p
    r-a-qu-e-t
    b-a-t
    s-k-i-pp-i-ng r-o-pe

Variation

- If you need team leaders in the lesson you could segment the names of children in the class who will then be team leaders.

Cross-curricular link

PE: games.

Rhythm and rhyme

Play a marching game as you practise your rhymes with this rap.

Suitable for

Children who are learning graphemes with more than one letter.

Aims

To hear and construct rhymes.

Resources

- Space to march around
- A drum or tambourine

What to do

- Ask the children to sit in a space and then listen to your rhyme:

  This is the rhythm
  This is the rhyme
  Here comes (someone)
  Marching in time.

  Say it again several times, letting them join in.
- Now ask them to stand up and march around in time to the rhythm, saying the rhyme as they do so. They should listen carefully because this time, instead of saying 'someone', you will be saying one of their names. At the end of the rhyme they should all stand still.

- Play the beat on the drum or tambourine to help the children march around in time. All say the rhyme as they march, then you choose a child:

    This is the rhythm
    This is the rhyme
    Here comes Elsa
    Marching in time.

- Now say:

    Choose two words
    To make a rhyme.

    Elsa chooses any two rhyming words to tell to the class.
- You now say:

    Yes, you did it
    You made a rhyme.

- Then start again with the rhyme and the marching.

Variation

- The child who has just chosen the two rhyming words could choose the next person at the right moment in the rhyme.

Cross-curricular link

PE: dance.

Is this my home?

Play a game about creatures and their homes.

Suitable for

Children who are learning graphemes with more than one letter.

Aims

To encourage the children to practise their oral blending and segmenting.

Resources

- For the Variation you will need to prepare split sentences on cards. Write out the following sentences before cutting each card into three sections as marked:

    A mouse (louse) / lives in / a house.

    A mole (vole, Old King Cole, foal) / lives in / a hole.

    A cat (rat, Pat) / sits on / a mat.

    A frog (dog, hog, Mog) / is near / a log.

What to do

- Tell the children that you want them to listen very carefully as you sound out some words.
  Say to them, *A m-ou-se lives in a h-ou-se*. Who can tell you what you said?
  Let several children have a turn at telling you.
  What do they notice about *house* and *mouse*? They rhyme.
- Can they think of another tiny little thing that rhymes with h-ou-se? Give clues until they tell you '*a louse*'. Then say, *A l-ou-se lives in a h-ou-se*.
- Repeat the process with the other sentences.

- Now play a game.
  Ask the children to find a space to sit in. You segment the name of a home, e.g. *m-a-t*.
- Remind the children that they must choose a character that rhymes with the home, e.g. *cat, rat, Pat*.
- The children now respond by miming the actions of any of those characters, e.g. wash their whiskers as a cat, scamper around like a rat or drive a post van like Pat.
- You then say, 'Go back home everyone', and they all find their space and sit down ready for the next clue.

Variation

- The children can use the sections of split sentences. They should put them together and read the sentence they have made to an adult, or write it and add a drawing.

Cross-curricular link

English: drama.

What can we do?

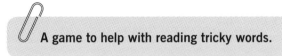

A game to help with reading tricky words.

Suitable for

Children who are learning graphemes with more than one letter.

Aims

To practise the words 'he', 'she' and 'we'.

Resources

- Three cards with large writing saying:
  He can ...
  She can ...
  We can ...

What to do

- Show the children the three cards and ask them to read them with you.
- Point out that the first word on each card ends with the letter 'e'. They also rhyme.
- Now explain the game to the children. They will move around the room to the music and when it stops you will say, 'Who can be a monkey?' Then you will hold up one of the cards.
  If you hold up '*He can ...*' the boys can jump about like monkeys and the girls will all say 'He can be a monkey' and point to a boy.
  If you hold up '*She can ...*' the girls will be the monkeys and the boys will say, 'She can be a monkey' and point to a girl.
  If you hold up '*We can ...*' everyone is a monkey and you all say together 'We can be monkeys'.
- Practise with each card in turn and then start the game.
- Dance around the room in between each request.
- You could try lots of animals – farm, jungle or pets.

Variation

- Link it to some work on feelings and ask, 'Who can be happy?' Or sad? scared? etc., and let the children show each emotion by their facial expressions and body language.

Cross·curricular link

PE: responding to stimuli.

Join the gang

An active game for the whole class to play in a large space.

Suitable for

Children who are learning graphemes of more than one letter.

Aims

To help children identify and remember rhyming words ending with the phoneme /ng/.

Resources

- A drum
- Four large pieces of card labelled 'bang', 'king', 'song' and 'lung'

What to do

- Ask the children to listen to the words *bang* and *gang*. What do they notice about the words? Yes, they are rhyming words.
- Hold up the card showing the word 'bang'. Can anyone identify the ending phoneme? Take a few moments to think of some other words that rhyme and try making up some nonsense words too.
- Explain to the children that there are other words that end with /ng/ that have a different vowel. Hold up the card 'king' and collect a few ideas for rhyming words with this word.
- Now tell the children about the game. First they run around the space and when you bang the drum they stop and sit down in groups of three or four.
  This is when you join a gang!
- Explain that you will then hold up a word and everyone in the gang must think of a word that rhymes, so they need to work together to make sure everyone in their gang has a different word. Then they

must sit quietly and wait. The members of each gang call out their rhyming word in turn when you ask.

- Play the game. When you bang the drum hold up the word 'bang' then allow time for the gang members to talk together before everyone has the chance to call out their word.
- Tell the children they must join a different gang each time you play. When you bang the drum hold up a different word that ends with /ng/.
- Declare which gang is the winner after listening to their rhyming words. Maybe the gang who spoke most clearly or the gang with a word no one else has thought of.

Variation

- As the children become more practised at remembering rhyming words you can increase the pace of the game by only asking one gang to call out their words. You could also make the game more challenging by asking the children to write down their rhyming words when they are in their gang.

Cross-curricular link

PE: working as a team.

Chapter 11
Stage C

Meal times

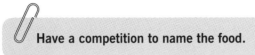

Have a competition to name the food.

Suitable for

Children who are learning alternative graphemes.

Aims

To create a fun way of discriminating between 'ee' and 'ea'.

Resources

- Paper and pencils
- Two large sheets of paper and a marker pen

What to do

- This is a useful activity to do at the start of some work on food, as it will provide the children with a word bank for other written activities.
- Do this as a whole class activity. Start with the children sitting at their own tables.
- Challenge the children to find as many food items as possible with the /ee/ phoneme in them.
- Allow a fixed time for the children to draw up their initial list.
- Now go round the class. Ask the first table to name one of their items. If any other table has it, they raise their hands, and each of these tables gets one point. If no one else has it, they get two points. You now ask the second table to name a food. Score points as before. They can't call out anything that has already been named.
- Continue round and round the tables until all the suggestions have been named.

- The children should then tally their scores and give a clap to the table with the most points.
- Have two large sheets of paper: one headed 'ee' and the other 'ea'.
- Ask one child to come out and write one of their foods on the correct paper. Their team members can help them with the spelling. Continue like this, taking one child from each table in turn until you have collated all their ideas.
- Leave the papers out for future reference.
  Some ideas: *cheese, sweets, green cabbage, leeks, beetroot, beef, seeds, Weetabix, coffee, toffee; cream, wheat, peach, beans, peas, tea-cake*.
  If any child suggests 'brie', explain that this is a French word and therefore has the French way of spelling this sound.

Variation

- Give each child a paper plate and let them draw onto it a meal made entirely of /ee/ foods.

Cross-curricular link

Science: food.

Could you? Would you?

Everyone thinks up a dilemma then discusses if they could, should or would do it!

Suitable for

Children who are learning alternative graphemes.

Aims

To develop children's spelling of three tricky words – could, should and would

Resources

- Paper and card to make a class book

What to do

- Write a sentence on the board then ask the children if they can identify the word that says 'could'.
- Explain that 'could' is a tricky word that only has three phonemes – /c/ /oul/ /d/ – but has a difficult spelling pattern. Point out that 'could' rhymes with 'should' and 'would' and list these on the board so that the children can see that all three words share the same spelling pattern for their ending.
- Ask the children to try to explain the meaning of these words. They are used to discuss future intentions. Tell the children you will give them an example:
  'Someone has kicked the ball over the fence into the garden next door.'
  Let's consider what they might do next.
  Could they climb over the fence to get it? (Is the fence low enough or strong enough?)
  Should they climb over the fence? (Is it the right thing to do?)

Would they climb over the fence? (Maybe the neighbours have said it's okay, or maybe they're just feeling a bit mischievous and decide to do it anyway.)

- Ask the children to think up situations in which you can use these three words to guess what happens next.
  Here are some suggestions:

  Dive in a lake
  Eat a snail
  Jump out of a window
  Climb a tree
  Kiss a frog.

- Make a class book with split pages. You only need three top-half pages for the three phrases:

  Could you?
  Should you?
  Would you?

  The children then draw the situation ideas, e.g. kiss a frog, with a written label beneath. Use these as the bottom-half pages of the book, and make as many of these as you like.
  Read each of the three top-half pages in turn so that each situation can be considered three ways before turning to the next illustrated half page.

Variation

- If you have a specific issue in school you can use this as a focus for the discussion, e.g. playtime rules.

Cross-curricular link

PSHE: considering moral and social dilemmas.

Think of a word

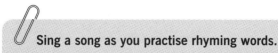

Sing a song as you practise rhyming words.

Suitable for

Children who are learning alternative graphemes.

Aims

To develop children's understanding of spelling variations in some rhyming words.

What to do

- Use the tune from 'Here we go round the mulberry bush' to sing:

    *Think of a word that rhymes with **snow***
    *Rhymes with **snow***
    *Rhymes with **snow***
    *Think of a word that rhymes with **snow***
    And say it out aloud.

- Repeat the song, allowing each child in the group to suggest a rhyming word – tell them it's okay to repeat words.
- Ask the children to remember the words suggested and write these on the board, e.g. *hoe, toe, mow, show, flow, row, sew, below, although, know, no, espresso, cappuccino.*
- Discuss the different spelling patterns. How many can you find with this final phoneme /o/?
- Perhaps you could extend this search by considering how this phoneme is written within words too?

Variation

- Choose other rhyming words that illustrate a variety of graphemes, for example 'blue' (shoe, grew).

Cross-curricular link

English: spelling patterns.

Full·time

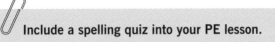

Include a spelling quiz into your PE lesson.

Suitable for

Children who are learning alternative graphemes.

Aims

To help children remember words spelt with 'ch' and words spelt with 'tch'.

Resources

- The hall or outdoor space, PE benches, sponge ball
  /ch/ words on individual cards in a suitable container
- Score board: labelled with the names of the two villages

What to do

- Introduce the game to the children, explaining that they will be spelling as well as playing a team game. Extra points can be scored if they can spell some match-related words.
- Tell them that they are the sports teams from two villages – *Much Marsh* and *Hitchford*.
  Can they think why you have chosen these names? Point out the two ways of spelling the sound /ch/, 'ch' and 'tch', and that one appears in each village name.
- Place the benches down opposite sides of the available space. Divide the children into two teams and ask them to sit on the benches, facing each other.
  The idea of the game is to keep the ball in the air and try to score a goal by getting it over the heads of the opposing team.

- If a team scores they get one point. They can double this if they can spell a word from a card chosen at random by the opposite team. Cards can be replaced in the container to keep the game going longer. This also helps to reinforce the spellings.
- Try to keep the words on the match/sport theme, e.g. *match, catch, cheering, championship, fetch, chipped, charity, watched, each, pitch, stitch, chance*.

Variation

- Use the words for report writing later. Start by creating phrases around them, e.g. *the crowd was cheering*, and then use them in a longer piece of writing.

Cross-curricular link

PE: ball games.

The silver sceptre

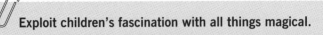

Exploit children's fascination with all things magical.

Suitable for

Children who are learning alternative graphemes.

Aims

To help the children sort out three ways to spell the /s/ sound.

Resources

- A cardboard 'sceptre' covered in silver paper
- Three containers, each with a label attached to the front of it: these could be pieces of coloured card cut out to represent ruby red, emerald green and sapphire blue. Onto these write the three graphemes 'ce', 'sce' and 's'
- Word cards of a selection of words beginning 'ce', 'sce' and 's', e.g.
  - *centipede, centimetre, certain, celebrity, cellar, celery, cereals, ceremony, celebration, century, ceiling*
  - *sceptre, scene, science, scent, scenery*
  - *silver, see, sailor, sandwich, sunny, sister, sock*

What to do

- Place the three baskets in front of the group of children and ask them to look at the three graphemes. Start with the 's' and ask them to read it to you and tell you what it says. Explain that the other two can also make this same sound in some words.
- Explain to the children that you have got a lot of words that all start with the sound /s/ but that they could be spelt in any of these three ways. Their task is to try to sort them out.
- Read one of the words to the group, making sure that no one can see the card. Who thinks they know which of the three graphemes is used in this word? Choose a child to come out, take the silver

sceptre and point to the basket it goes in. You put it in there, still not letting the children see it – whether it is the right answer or not. Continue in this way until all the cards are in the baskets.

- Now take one of the baskets. Take the cards out and show them, one at a time, to the children. Each time read it to them, encouraging them to read along with you. Then ask them if it is in the right basket. Now put it in the right place.
- Do the same with each basket in turn until all of the cards are in the right baskets. These baskets of words can now be used as part of your word bank.

Variation

- Children can create some captions using as many /s/ words from the baskets as they can, and any others they can think of, and illustrate them, e.g.
  The silver centipede ate all of the celery.
  The sailor went to a celebration party.
  The ceiling was sparkling with silvery stars.

Cross-curricular link

Science: materials.

Rhyming colours

Ask the children to choose rhyming colour words.

Suitable for

Children who are learning alternative graphemes.

Aims

To encourage children to hear rhymes and explore a range of alternative graphemes.

Resources

- Simple dictionaries

What to do

- Work with a group of children sitting together.
- Tell them you want them to think of rhyming words.
  Discuss what makes a word rhyme – it's when the endings of two words sound the same.
  Can anyone give you an example?
  Explain that the game involves thinking of a colour that rhymes with whatever you choose.
- Ask 'What colour is my bed?'
  Tell the children they must think of a colour that rhymes with bed – (red). Write the word **bed** on the board.
- 'What colour is my shoe?' – (blue). Write the word **shoe**.
  'What colour is my elbow?' – (yellow). Write the word **elbow**.
  'What colour is my sink?' – (pink). Write the word **sink**.
- Ask the children to use the dictionaries to find the spellings of the colour words that rhyme with the words on the board. They are looking for red/blue/yellow/pink.

- Compare the spelling of the colour to its rhyming word.
  Can they find which colour word doesn't share the same spelling pattern as its rhyming word?
- Next time you play, ask questions about a sack (black), a crown (brown), a kite (white) and a bean (green).

Variation

- The children can write sentences using the items mentioned and their rhyming colour words, e.g. *My elbow is yellow because I put it in the custard*.

Cross-curricular link

English: rhyming words.

Bloo? Blue? Blew?

 Compete in groups to win the homophone quiz.

Suitable for

Children who are learning alternative phonemes.

Aims

To involve children in reading and choosing the correct spelling.

Resources

- A set of word cards for each table. Use words that you are currently learning where there are two words that sound the same but are spelt differently (homophones). Then add a rogue third option – phonically plausible but *incorrect*, e.g.

  blue, blew, bloo
  shoo, shoe, shew
  fort, fought, faught
  bare, bear, bair
  stair, stare, stear
  fete, fate, fait

What to do

- Tell the children that they are going to be competing in the quiz as a table. They should choose one person from their table to be the captain – this person will hold up the answer that everyone has agreed on. Then they should choose one person to keep the score. This person will need a paper and pencil.
- Hand out a set of cards to each table. The children should spread these out so that everyone can read them.
- Explain to the children that you are going to say a word, followed by a sentence with that word in it. They should choose the card with

that word on it and, when you say so, the captain will hold up the
card. Tell them that there are three options for each word.

- You will tell each table whether they are right or not. If they are
  right they get a point.
- They should put the card back into play in case they got it wrong
  and will need it again.
- The winner is the table with the most points and they will go out to
  play first.
- Some ideas for sentences:
  - *The wind blew the tree down.*
  - *Mary lost her shoe.*
  - *The soldiers fought a long battle.*
  - *The grizzly bear roared.*
  - *Don't stare at the old lady.*
  - *The school fete is on Saturday.*
  - *The flag was red, white and blue.*
  - *As the goose came near, Tom shouted 'Shoo!'*
  - *There was a creak on the stair.*
  - *The bare branches of the tree swayed in the wind.*
  - *They were stuck! What would their fate be?*
  - *The soldiers were in the fort.*

Variation

- If you use this with a small group of children they could have a complete set
  of cards each – choose only three or four homophones for this. When you
  say the sentence they turn their first answer card over. When they find the
  second answer they place it face down on top of the first one. Continue for
  about six sentences. Tidy the unused cards away. Keep the cards in the pile
  in order. You can then ask them to turn over one card at a time and you can
  tell them 'right' or 'wrong'. The children should keep hold of the right answers
  to total their score.

Cross-curricular link

English: group discussion.

Nine knights

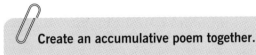 **Create an accumulative poem together.**

Suitable for

Children who are learning alternative graphemes.

Aims

To encourage the children to use alternative graphemes for the phoneme /n/.

Resources

- Dictionaries

What to do

- Explain to the children that you are going to make a poem where every line is longer than the one before it, and most words should begin with /n/. The first line has only one word: *Knights*.
- The second line has two words: *Nine knights*.
- Can anyone suggest what those knights might be doing for line three? E.g. *Nine knights kneeling (or knitting, nibbling)*.
- Line four tells us where they were doing it. Has anyone got a suggestion? E.g. *Nine knights kneeling next to a gnome*.
- Continue in this way, making a longer and longer sentence each time. Keep repeating what went before, line by line. Make it as long as you choose.
- The children can now have a go at writing this poem, or a similar one, for themselves. Remind them that the /n/ phoneme can be spelt in several ways. If you have been working on this they may be familiar with 'n', 'gn', 'kn'. As they write they should check their spelling in the dictionaries using these three options to help them.

Variation

- For less able children, start them with: *trees; tall trees; ten tall trees.* This phoneme is spelt consistently with the grapheme 't' (unless they add Thomas!).

Cross-curricular link

English: poetry.

Crunch, munch

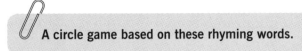

A circle game based on these rhyming words.

Suitable for

Children who are learning alternative graphemes.

Aims

To help children notice two phonemes for the grapheme 'ch'.

What to do

- Sit in a circle. Tell the children that they are going to learn a new rhyme.
- Explain that the last line is a question that they can take turns answering.
- Teach them the rhyme:

    Crunch, munch
    Crunch, munch
    What are you eating for lunch?

- You might like to try this out a few times, with everyone repeating the rhyme and children suggesting any food stuff they like as an answer.
- Now write the three words '*crunch, munch, lunch*' for the children to see and ask who notices some letters that are the same in all three words.

    Ask the children what sound you hear at the end of these words – it's /sh/.

    (It may be appropriate to explain that when an 'n' comes before 'ch' in a word it is usually pronounced /sh/, e.g. pinch and punch.)

- Now ask the children what sound you would usually expect from the letters 'ch'?

    Can anyone think of a food that begins with the /ch/ phoneme?

    Repeat the rhyme and encourage the first child to offer a suggestion.

- Continue round the circle until everyone has offered a suggestion. It might be appropriate to accept repeated answers if the children find this challenging or it's the first time you've played the game. Suggestions could include: *chocolate, chips, chops, cheese, cheesy straws, chipolatas, cherries, chicken, cheddar, chapatti, chewing gum!*

Variation

- The children say the 'Crunch munch' rhyme but the adult segments the /ch/ words for them to identify, e.g. ch-ee-se, ch-ew-i-ng g-u-m.

Cross-curricular link

DT: food.

High in the sky

Create rhyming sentences and explore the different ways of spelling /igh/.

Suitable for

Children who are learning alternative graphemes.

Aims

To encourage children to discover alternative graphemes for the phoneme /igh/.

Resources

- For the variation: coloured pens and white paper

What to do

- Ask the children to help you think of words that rhyme with *high*.
- Let the children take turns making suggestions.
  See how many you can collect.
- As you write the words on the board encourage the children to notice how the phoneme /igh/ is spelt in the words.
  Examples might include: *my, sigh, why, cry, eye, reply, tie, goodbye.*
- Now ask the children to help you think of words that rhyme with *night*.
- Let the children take turns making suggestions.
  See how many you can collect.
- As you write the words on the board encourage the children to notice how the phoneme /igh/ is spelt in the words.
  Examples might include: *bright, white, write, height, light, polite.*

- Read the words together and suggest some phrases that illustrate the words as you read them, e.g.

  Pie in the sky.

  Hold tight on the flight.

  I spy with my little eye.

  I say goodbye as you fly by.

- Divide the children into pairs and ask them to choose words from the lists to write some rhyming phrases.
- Take some time at the end of the session to listen to the children's ideas.

Variation

- If you want to create a display of their work, ask the children to write their rhyming phrases with coloured pens on white cloud shapes and display these on sky-blue backing paper.

Cross-curricular link

English: wordplay.

What's in the toy box?

Develop the children's oral blending and segmenting skills using toys.

Suitable for

Children who are learning alternative graphemes.

Aims

To give children practice with oral blending and segmenting a range of words.

Resources

- Toys from around the classroom, e.g. book, doll, train, ball, car, teddy, hoop, beanbag, jigsaw, rope, cubes, flag

What to do

- Hide some toys in a box or basket.
- Collect together a small group of children.
- Explain that they are going to guess what is in the toy box.
- Lift the lid and let the first child feel in the box for a toy, without revealing what it is to anyone else.
- Ask them to segment the name of the toy, e.g. *t-r-ai-n*.
- Encourage the other children to use their oral blending skills to work out what toy it is.
- Choose the next child to feel in the toy box and continue until everyone has had a turn.

Variation

- At the end of the game the children can attempt to write down the toys they identified. This will provide an opportunity for assessment of the children's ability to spell a range of phonemes.

Cross-curricular link

PSHE: developing relationships through play.

Verb or noun

A team game that encourages children to write a range of words and understand the labels of verb or noun.

Suitable for

Children who are learning alternative graphemes.

Aims

To encourage children to identify words as verbs or nouns and to practise spelling a range of graphemes.

Resources

- Two colours of strips of paper long enough for children's sentences
- A list of words that can be verbs or nouns, e.g. *paint, wash, wish, plant, dance, curl, slide, dress, walk, spy, fly*

What to do

- Divide the children into two teams: verbs and nouns.
  (There should be no more than six in each team.)
- Remind the children that verbs are action words and nouns name things.
  Ask the children for examples of verbs and nouns.
- Explain to them that in this game the words can be either verbs or nouns.
  Illustrate this with one example, *paint*:
  I like to paint – uses the word '*paint*' as a verb.
  The red paint is best – uses the word '*paint*' as a noun.
  (It may be appropriate to illustrate more examples from the list.)

- When the children are ready to play, explain the game.
  - A word will be segmented aloud by the adult.
  - The members of each team then work together to decide on a sentence using the word in its appropriate form for their team.
  - One member of the team is then nominated to write the sentence on a strip of paper.
  - Another member reads the sentence, checks the word is spelt correctly, then takes the finished sentence to the front.
  - Both team members read their sentence aloud to make sure the word is used as a verb or a noun, as required by their team.
  - Now the spelling of the written word is checked in both sentences.
  - Whichever team arrived first at the front with a correctly written sentence wins the point.

  (Decide if the other words need to be spelt correctly as well to gain the point.)
- Continue playing with 11 words, then declare the winning team.

Variation

- To make the game easier the words can be printed on the board as the adult segments the word. The teams then only have to decide how to use the word in the sentence.

Cross-curricular link

English: language structure.

Have fun with tricky words

When children are struggling with strange spellings, appeal to their sense of humour.

Suitable for

Children who are practising alternative graphemes.

Aims

To help children who are finding it difficult to remember unusual spellings.

Resources

- Strips of paper, card and felt-tip pens (for the third idea, below)

What to do

A series of ideas for you to use:

- One approach is to draw attention to the strange spelling. You can mis-pronounce words such as *biscuit*, say the 'u', so *bis-cu-it,* or the 'c' in *scissors*, so *s-c-issors*. Make a joke of it and let the children correct your pronunciation.
- Make up a silly sentence using the letters of the word as initial sounds, e.g. *big elephants can always understand smaller elephants = because*.
- If children are struggling with a word, such as *'people'*, ask them to create their own silly sentence. Write the word across the page with each letter well spaced out. Write the silly sentence words on individual strips of paper that can be glued on, coming down from each letter of the word. Because you want the children to focus on 'people', it's important that the focus word remains correctly aligned, left to right across the page. This is not an acrostic poem. Children could write in felt-tip pen on cards, and add a picture. They can then be displayed for future reference.

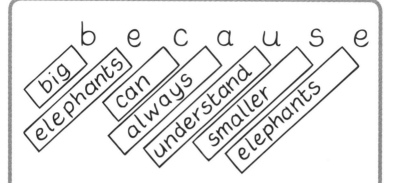

- To clarify the use of the two spellings of '*there/their*', try this simple explanation.

  Write out both words clearly. As the children watch you, change the dot above the 'i' to a circle and create a smiley face inside it. When they want to say, for example, their shoes, their friends, their house, the word 'their' is referring to people. So they should use the 'their' with the smiley face.

  The other 'there' is for places as in here and where (see activity *Where the Wild Things Are* on page 62).

Variation

- Try using word searches, crosswords, etc. from a range of published quiz books and magazines. Tear out the pages and leave a selection available for those odd spare moments.

Cross-curricular link

English: tricky words.

Chapter 12
Stage D

Find the schwa

A teacher-led session to investigate this sound of many spellings!

Suitable for

Children who are gaining confidence with spelling.

Aims

To help the children recognise the sound and consider some of its spellings.

What to do

- Children like a new word – especially one that their parents may not know.
- Write the symbol ə on the whiteboard and tell the children that this is a 'schwa'. Let everyone have a go at saying this new word.
- Next, make the sound and let the children try making it.
- Now explain to the children that you are going to say a word with a schwa in it. They should listen carefully and tell you which part of the word is the schwa.
  Say a word, e.g. *doctor*. Children should identify that the schwa is at the end.
- Write the word on the board with the children's help. Can anyone underline the schwa part? This is 'or'.
- Repeat this with, for example, *mother, pillar, picture, thorough, centre, murmur, favour*.
- Who notices anything about this list of words? The children should be able to tell you that every time they have marked the schwa, it has been a different spelling.

Variation

- Choose a child to come out and segment any one of the words on the board. The others should raise their hands when they know which one it is. If they get it right they can segment the next word.

Cross-curricular link

English: spelling tricky words.

Arctic friends

Children make a lift-the-flap book to practise their spelling and reading.

Suitable for

Children who are gaining confidence with spelling.

Aims

To provide a fun way to think about sounds that rhyme with /air/ and to spell them correctly.

Resources

- Each child needs two sheets of A4 paper, folded in half and stapled to make a book
- Scraps of paper and glue or tape to make the flaps
- Large picture of a polar bear in its natural environment
- Optional: Foster, J. (ed) (2003) *Completely Crazy Poems*, London: Collins
- Photocopies of the words of the poem 'Elephants' by Kaye Umansky

What to do

- Show the children the picture of the polar bear and ask them to tell you what it is. Explain that they are going to think about the word 'bear'. Can they spell it in this context? Children can come out and write it on a whiteboard, or write it on their individual boards.
- Read the poem 'Elephants' (Kaye Umansky) to the children. The second verse uses 'polar bear' and then 'polar bare'. When the children have stopped laughing, write both of these down and point out the two different spellings for the two different meanings.

- Give the children a photocopy of these words:

  On the freezing ice, the polar bear
  Was moving here and moving there,
  Then stops and stands to stare ...
  What's there?

- Read it together and then ask for suggestions. What was there? Only suggestions that rhyme with /air/ can be accepted. E.g. pear, chair, hair, mare.
- Once you have collected a lot of words, tell the children that they are going to make a lift-the-flap book. They will stick the photocopy on the first page and illustrate it. On each following page they should write one of the /air/ words and make a cloud shape to go over it. They will draw the picture of the object on the cloud before sticking it in place.

Variation

- Create a fabric collage of a polar bear and surround him with /air/ words.

Cross-curricular link

Science: changing materials (ice/water).

Bark and spell!

An assessment activity to monitor the children's phoneme/grapheme knowledge.

Suitable for

Children who are gaining confidence with spelling.

Aims

To provide a fun way to find out if the children have an understanding of alternative spelling options.

Resources

- A large picture of a dog (or other chosen animal)

What to do

- Use this activity as an assessment tool. Which children can remember, and correctly use, the various graphemes for the three phonemes /w/, /u/ and /f/?
- Show the children the picture of the dog. What noise do dogs make? When a dog barks we usually describe the sound as 'woof'. Can the children tell you the three phonemes that make up this word?
- Once you have established /w/ /u/ /f/, as the three phonemes, ask the children to make a list of different ways they could spell the word 'woof'. Don't remind them of the usual way of spelling it. Encourage them to see this as fun, and not a test of their spelling accuracy.
- Here are some ideas, but your children might find more: woof, wooff; wuf, wuff; whuf, whuff; wough, whough; whoof, whooff; wooph, wuph; whuph, whooph.
  If this is part of a teaching session rather than as assessment activity, the children could work in pairs.

- Collate your results and then use them to create a display.
- Place a picture, photo or collage of a barking dog in the centre of your display area. Write the optional spellings of 'woof' in speech bubbles and arrange them around the picture. Make a title, 'My dog says ...'.

Variation

- Adapt the idea for other animal sounds: try a cow or a cat, a horse or a donkey.

Cross-curricular link

Art: animals in art.

Try:

Las Meninas by Velazquez (1656)

Mr and Mrs Andrews by Gainsborough (1750)

Sunday Afternoon on the Island of Grande Jatte by Seurat (1886)

Boy with a Dog by Picasso (1905)

Maurice by Andy Warhol (1976)

Stanley by David Hockney (1990)

'A weird world'

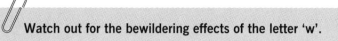

Watch out for the bewildering effects of the letter 'w'.

Suitable for

Children who are gaining confidence with spelling.

Aims

To raise the children's awareness of the unusual effect of the letter 'w' as they read.

Resources

- A copy of the poem below, large enough for the group to read:

    'A weird world'

    A whiskery whelk who was wandering
    Met old Walter Wall, who was wondering,
    Do wolves wear white?
    Can a wasp learn to write?
    And do whales go to Wales for the night?

What to do

- Tell the children that you are going to read them a poem. Read it out and let them enjoy it.
- Now show them your large copy of it, and ask them to join in as you read it together.
- Ask them which letter is at the start of a lot of the words. They should spot the 'w'.
- Tell them that it is a very strange letter because it often can be seen but not heard. It is also known to have a peculiar effect on the vowels 'a' and 'o' when they follow it. You have to listen carefully as you read in order to see this.

- Tell the children that they are going to work with a partner to look carefully at any one of the 'w' words in the poem, and see if they can find out something peculiar that it is doing. Give them one example to explain what you mean. Choose from one of these facts:
  - It can be followed by an 'h' that you don't hear, as in 'whales'.
  - It can be silent itself so that you wouldn't know it was there, as in 'write'.
  - It changes the vowel sounds of 'a' and 'o' from what you would expect them to be, as in 'wall' and 'wolves'.
- Allow the children a few minutes to come up with their own example.
- Now go through the rhyme, stopping at each initial 'w'. Ask the children if anyone spotted something about this word. They now tell the group about their strange 'w'.
- Continue through the whole poem, asking for anyone to contribute if there is a word that no one actually chose.
- The children could then try to invent new questions with at least one strange 'w' effect, for lines three and four of the poem. This is best done as an oral activity.

  Here are some additional words that the children could choose from: *wool, woolly; wrinkled; wrap, wrapped, wrapping paper; whisper; whirlpool; warm; worm; whiffy; whoops; worse; wreck; wrist; waddle; waffle; washing.*

Variation

- The children could write some 'whacky questions', as long or as short as they like, using the above words.

Cross·curricular link

English: poetry.

What a difference one letter can make!

A lively game where actions depend on decoding carefully.

Suitable for

Children who are gaining confidence with spelling.

Aims

To help the children appreciate the need to decode words carefully.

Resources

- A set of cards with one of the three words 'fried', 'fiend' or 'friend' printed on individual cards. It makes the game easier if you print the words in different-coloured inks: one for 'fried', one for 'fiend' and another for 'friend'
- An open space in which to play the game

What to do

- Show the children the word 'friend' and ask who can read the word. (It may be appropriate to discuss that the /e/ phoneme is spelt with the letters 'ie'.)
- Now tell the children you are going to show them another word that has only one letter that is different but is quite different in meaning and pronunciation.
- Show the children the word 'fiend'.
  Can anyone read the word? What letter is missing?
  (It may be appropriate to discuss that 'ie' creates the /ee/ phoneme in this word.)
- Now tell the children that the last word you are going to show has just one letter different from the word 'friend' but again is quite different in pronunciation and meaning.

- Show the children the word 'fried'.
  Can anyone read the word? What letter is missing?
  (It may be appropriate to discuss that 'i' creates the /igh/ phoneme in this word and 'e' is part of the suffix 'ed'.)
- Shuffle the cards and read the three words again, then encourage the children to focus on the 'r' and the 'n' to aid quick recognition of the words.
- Ask the children to sit in a circle. Put the pile of cards in the centre and explain that the words will be mixed up in the central pile. Explain that one child comes to the centre and turns over the top card, then reads the word aloud.
  If the word is 'friend' everyone shakes hands with someone nearby.
  If the word is 'fried' they jump about on the spot.
  If the word is 'fiend' the child in the centre becomes the fiend so everyone runs away from the circle and the child who read the card has to catch someone.
  The child who is caught then takes over reading the cards.

Variation

- To play a quieter version of the game, when the child reads the word 'fiend' he just changes places with someone and they take their turn in the centre reading the cards.

Cross-curricular link

English: wordplay.

This week's challenge is ...

Modify this game each week as the children test their general knowledge as well as their phonics.

Suitable for

Children who are gaining confidence with spelling.

Aims

To set the children an ongoing challenge to reflect their awareness of spellings.

Resources

- A grid that can be adapted each week
  Start with a large piece of paper divided into six columns
  Add a heading for each column, e.g. *girls' names, boys' names, towns, football teams, colours, animals, plants, cartoon figures, countries, something you'd find in a house*
  Make a title with the last word missing: *'This week's challenge is ...'*; you will attach a separate grapheme there each week

What to do

- Choose a grapheme that you have been working on, e.g. 'ow'. Attach it to the title.
- Read this with the children, reminding them that the challenge is to find words that contain the grapheme that can go into any of the categories listed at the tops of the columns, e.g. 'ow': *Rowena, brown, brown bear, bowl, Grimsby Town, Cowdenbeath, Carlow, towel*.
- Children complete the grid over the week as they think of, or come across, words. Remind the children that there won't always be something for each column, and some columns may have many more words than others.

- At the end of each week, sit together and read through the list. Do you always pronounce the grapheme in the same way? Use this as a discussion point.

Variation

- You could use phonemes rather than graphemes if your children are familiar with the way of writing these for the title, e.g. /igh/.

Cross-curricular link

Geography: places.

Press the rewind button

 A game to encourage children to add the prefix 'un'.

Suitable for

Children who are gaining confidence with spelling.

Aims

To provide an opportunity for children to add the prefix 'un' to a range of verbs.

Resources

- A set of cards with a verb printed on each card
  Choose verbs where it's possible to reverse the action, e.g. *do, wind, bolt, fasten, cover, buckle, load, wrap, clip, twist, bend, tie*
- A horn or buzzer for the rewind button

What to do

- Sit in a circle with the children and explain that they will take it in turns to select a word from the middle of the circle.
- Read all the words together then spread them on the floor inside the circle.
- Ask what type of words are included in this game – *verbs, describing actions*.
- Explain that when it's their turn to pick up a card they must then return to their place and tell everyone a sentence using that word, e.g. 'I fasten my coat', or 'I fasten my shoe'.
- Practise taking turns to pick up a card and say the word in a sentence.
- When the children are confident with this part of the game, explain that sometimes you will press the rewind button.
  Demonstrate the noise!
  If you don't want to make a noise, simply say *rewind*.

- Discuss what happens when you rewind something. (If necessary, demonstrate how the action is reversed with an appropriate video clip on the internet.)
- Tell the children when they hear this noise they must rewind the last action.
  So if a child has just picked up the word *pack* and the rewind button is pressed, they must make a sentence that reverses the action – 'I unpack my bag'.
- Play the game, using the rewind button as often as you like.

Variation

- At the end of the game the children can use some of the words to write two opposite sentences, using the verb and then with the 'un' prefix, e.g. *I fold the deck chair. I unfold the deck chair.*

Cross-curricular link

PSHE: participation in a game.

Guess the mime

A game where children read an adverb and mime an action in that way.

Suitable for

Children who are gaining confidence with spelling.

Aims

To provide an opportunity for children to read words with the suffix 'ly'.

Resources

- A set of cards with an adverb printed on each card, e.g. *slowly*, *quietly*, *loudly*, *sadly*, *suddenly*, *carefully*, *bravely*, *quickly*, *safely*, *tidily*, *gently*, *noisily*, *messily*

What to do

- Read the cards with the children and ask them what is the same in all these words – do they notice the 'ly' on each word?
- Explain that these are adverbs and their purpose is to describe the verb.
  Illustrate this with an example, e.g. *I shout **loudly***.
- Tell the children they are going to pick a card and choose an action that they can mime to see if the rest of the class can guess the adverb.
- Put the cards in a pile facing downwards and choose a child to have the first turn.
  Be ready with some ideas of actions they can mime in case you need to prompt them, e.g. pack their school bag, put on their shoes or open a door.
- It's helpful if the child announces what action they are miming before they start.
- Ask the children to put their hand up if they know the adverb and if the child chosen by the adult guesses the adverb correctly they take the next turn.

Variation

- One child is chosen to go outside the room for a few moments while the rest of the children in the group read the adverb. The child whose turn it is comes back into the group and can ask any number of children to demonstrate the adverb by performing various actions until they think they can guess the adverb.

Cross-curricular link

English: language structure.

Work it out

Set the children a challenge to find the rule for the initial sound /k/.

Suitable for

Children who are gaining confidence with spelling.

Aims

To challenge the children to investigate spelling by looking at the initial sound /k/.

Resources

- Whiteboard

What to do

- Tell the children that there are two letters of the alphabet that make the sound /k/. Can they remember what they are? ('c' and 'k'.)
- Now ask the children if they can tell you any simple words that start with the /k/ sound. The words should be only one syllable each, e.g. *come, keep*.
- As the children make their suggestions, write them down all over a whiteboard or large sheet of paper. Don't sort them into 'k' and 'c' words at this stage.
- Explain to the children that there is a rule about which of the two letters they should write for this one sound, when the words are only one syllable long. Can they discover it? They should work together with a partner discussing their ideas.
- Allow about five minutes for them to try to solve this. If necessary you may have to show them.
- First of all, list the words by initial grapheme. Then ask the children to look at the vowel that follows it.

- They should notice that:
  'c' is always followed by 'a', 'o' or 'u'.
  'k' is always followed by 'e' or 'i'.
  E.g.
      cat, cot, cut, kill, Ken
      can, colt, cup, kilt, Kent
      calf, comb, cube, keel, king
- The rule holds true for most common words, even some longer words such as *cushion, cucumber, catalogue, colander, kitchen, kennel*.

Variation

- Children could make a further list of words that have an initial 'k' that is silent, e.g. *knee*, *know*, *knife*, *knock*.

Cross-curricular link

PSHE: cooperating with others in a group task.

1, 2, 3, 4, go

Share your ideas in a circle game and then find out how many ways you can spell the phoneme /oa/.

Suitable for

Children who are gaining confidence with spelling.

Aims

To challenge the children to find out how many ways they might spell /oa/.

Resources

- Dictionaries

What to do

- The children should be sitting in a circle.
- Tell the children that you want them to think of words that contain the phoneme or sound /oa/. Explain that you will go round the circle repeating the sequence: 1, 2, 3, 4, /oa/ word, 1, 2, 3, 4, /oa/ word, etc.

  So, the first four children will be saying numbers and the fifth one will be saying a word.

  (If the number of children in your group divides equally by five, you need to use a count of six for this game, rather than four, so that everyone gets a chance to say a word.)
- Go round the circle, with the first child saying '1', the second saying '2', the third saying '3' and the fourth saying '4'. The fifth child (or seventh, depending on the number in your group) says a word with an /oa/ sound. Start counting again from the next child in the circle. Continue round and round the circle in this way, e.g. *1, 2, 3, 4, 'go', 1, 2, 3, 4, 'coat'*.

- Once your children have used this system to remember a lot of /oa/ words, explain the next part of their task.
- They should work with a partner to write down as many /oa/ words as they can remember. Then they should sort them into spelling families according to the way in which the /oa/ sound is written. How many ways can they find to spell this phoneme? We found 11: *go, toe, bow, road, gnome, yolk, although, brooch, doh, sew, shoulder*.

Variation

- Ask the children to work individually to write their lists and use this as an assessment activity.

Cross-curricular link

English: knowledge of spelling families.

All change

Changing words one letter at a time in a small group game.

Suitable for

Children who are gaining confidence with spelling.

Aims

To practise spelling simple words by focusing on individual letters.

Resources

- Sets of alphabet cards, as used in activity Rainbow games on pages 234–7

What to do

- Choose the cards you need for the starter word e.g. *cat*, and lay them out where everyone in the group can read them.
- Tell the children that you want to change this word into, for example, *dog*. Make that word up and set it out for the children to see.
- Now show them how this can be done, explaining your choices as you go along, e.g.
  'I am starting with *cat*.
  If I use the "o" from *dog* as the vowel I can make *cat* into *cot*.
  Now if I use the "d" from *dog* I can make *cot* into *dot*.
  Now I can use the "g" from *dog* to turn *dot* into *dog*.
  I did it in four words: *cat, cot, dot, dog.*'
- Ask the children to look carefully at the four words you have made. Explain to them that this isn't the only way it could be done. It might be done more ways or include more words to do it, but all the different ways would be right.

- Remove your example before setting the children the task of trying this for themselves. Remind them that they must only make real words as they do this. Let them have a go with a partner to change *cat* to *dog*.
- Once the children understand the process they could try some other words. If you are setting this, remember that the two words you choose should have the same number of letters in them!
  Try:
  boy to *man* – *boy, toy, top, mop, map, man*
  wet to *dry* – *wet, set, sat, say, day, dry.*

Variation

- It might help the children if you write the two words in a grid with a fixed number of changes, and perhaps a few letters given.

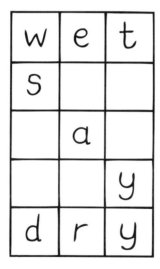

Cross-curricular link

English: wordplay.

'e' free

A writing activity that involves omitting a given letter.

Suitable for

Children who are gaining confidence with spelling.

Aims

To raise the children's awareness of the importance of different letters.

What to do

- Write the following sentence where everyone can see it:
  A cat was having a drink of milk from a brown cup.
- Ask the children to read it carefully and then tell you which vowel is missing. It's the 'e'.
- Tell them that you are going to write some more sentences without an 'e' in them. Who can suggest a starting point for the next one? E.g. *a dog, a crow, a man, an old woman.*
- Share the writing of a few individual sentences:
  A dog is barking.
  A cow is in a barn.
  An old man is at a bus stop.
  Two birds fly by.
- Then try writing two or three sentences that will form a miniature story. This is much harder than it first seems as 'e' is the most frequently used letter in English.
  Who or what is it about?
  An old woman.
  What was she doing?
  An old woman sat in a chair.
  Where was she?
  An old woman sat in a chair by a window.

Who was with her?
An old woman sat in a chair by a window. A brown dog is barking at a cat passing by.

- The children can now have a go at writing their own VERY short story of a few sentences without using a letter of your choosing. The most frequently used, and therefore the hardest to omit, are: e, t, a, i, n, o, s (this list is given in the order of greatest frequency).

Variation

- Try writing a sentence where every word starts with the same letter.

Cross-curricular link

English: wordplay.

Make it longer

Give the children a base word and challenge them to make it longer by adding prefixes and suffixes.

Suitable for

Children who are gaining confidence with spelling.

Aims

To encourage children to use prefixes and suffixes.

Resources

- Whiteboard and coloured pens

What to do

- Write the word *danger* on the board.
- Ask if anyone can read the word.
  Segment the word and discuss the spelling of the /j/ phoneme.
- Suggest some other words where the /j/ phoneme is spelt with a 'g'.
  E.g. *age, stage, orange, gentle, giant, angel*.
- Ask the children how many letters make up the word *danger*.
  Can anyone think of a sentence that contains the word danger?
- Tell the children you are going to make the word longer by adding a prefix.
  It may be appropriate to explain that a prefix is fixed to the beginning and a suffix is fixed to the end of a word.
- Write *endanger* on the board using a different coloured pen for the prefix. Does everyone understand what it means?
- Can anyone think how to make it even longer?
  Try adding the suffix '*ed*'.
  Can the children think of some animals that are an endangered species?

- Now ask the children to return to the word *danger* and make it longer in a different way.
  Prompt the children if necessary to try adding the suffix *'ous'*.
  Write the word *dangerous* on the board using a different coloured pen for the suffix.
  Can someone think of a sentence using the word *dangerous*?
- Ask if the children can make the word even longer by adding another suffix. Prompt them to try *'ly'* – *dangerously* and write this for them to see
  Ask for sentences that contain the word *dangerously*.
- Look at the new words you have made using prefixes and suffixes. Which word was the longest?
- Set the children to work in pairs to make a longer word by adding prefixes and suffixes to some other base words, e.g. *interest, kind, possible, truth, use.*

Variation

- When the children have completed this challenge look at all the different prefixes and suffixes they have used. How many other base words can they fix them to?

Cross-curricular link

English: vocabulary extension.

Make a new word

A game where children pick up a card and find a partner to make a new compound word.

Suitable for

Children who are gaining confidence with spelling.

Aims

To encourage children to read and use compound words.

Resources

- Print compound words on individual cards, e.g. *butterfly, motorway, afternoon, outside, bathroom, playtime, understand, policeman, midnight* (If you choose words that are interchangeable, such as *play, bath, room* and *time*, make sure you have combinations that work)

What to do

- Give out the cards, one between two children.
- Encourage everyone to read their compound word to the group.
- Ask the children to decide how to split their word into two words and let them cut each word into two.
- Drop the cut cards into a box.
- Ask the children to sit in a circle and pass the box around so that everyone can take a card.
- Now ask the children to find a partner whose word fits with theirs to make a compound word.
- The two children then sit together in the circle ready to show their word.
- Maybe you will decide to ask the children for a sentence that includes their word too.
- When everyone has read their compound word, return the cards to the box ready to play again.

Variation

- Challenge the children to think of other compound words and add those to the box.

Cross-curricular link

English: vocabulary extension.

Bingo

Collect together lots of difficult words all with the same initial phonemes, then as children play bingo they learn to blend and segment long and complicated words.

Suitable for

Children who are gaining confidence with spelling.

Aims

To encourage children to blend and segment polysyllabic words.

Resources

- Rectangles of card divided into a grid of six squares

What to do

- Write the word 'in' on the board and tell the children that lots of words begin with this prefix.
- Collect together suggestions.
  (It might be appropriate to set this as a homework challenge to see who can list the most words.)
- Discuss the meanings of the words and identify those that make an opposite by adding the prefix, e.g. *visible/invisible*.
- Practise oral blending and segmenting several of the words together.
- Write out six words on each bingo card (it doesn't matter if some are repeated).
  Here are 24 suggestions for your bingo cards: *interesting, intelligent, instantly, inspector, innocent, investigation, incorrectly, interactive, intercom, interfere, international, interpreter, interviewer, introduction, instruction, invitation, independent, inedible, invisible, incurable, inconvenient, inactivity, invalid, indirectly*.

- Give out the bingo cards, one to be shared between two or three children.
- Explain that you will segment the word and they must raise their hand when they have used their oral blending skills to identify the word on their card and that you will then choose one child to identify the word.
- Every group that has that word on their card can then cover it with a cube or sticker.
- The group that covers all six words first wins the game.

Variations

- More able children might like to write out the words to create the bingo cards and they may be able to create sentences that demonstrate the meaning of words when they have identified them.
- They could also be set the challenge of finding other words that have a prefix beginning with 'im', e.g. *impossible, impolite, improbable, imaginary, immigration, immense, improve*.

Cross-curricular link

English: vocabulary extension.

Guess the word

> **Challenge the children to use their decoding skills letter by letter.**

Suitable for

Children who are gaining confidence with spelling.

Aims

To remind the children of the importance of reading every letter in a word.

Resource

- Large cards with individual words written in clear print, with each letter separate from the rest. Try: *said, great, heart, half, danger, photo, shoe, shoulder*

What to do

- Explain to the children that you have some hidden words and that you want them to work out what they are.
- Hold one card facing the children, with a blank piece of card, the same size, to cover a word card. Pull the word card gently to the right to reveal one letter at a time.
- When the children can see the first letter of the word, ask them what sound it makes and to 'Guess the word'.
- Allow a few guesses, then reveal the second letter. Now what might the word be? Continue in this way until the whole word is visible.
- If you start with the word 'said', the children see 's' first and could guess many words. Some children might think of words where 's' is combined with another letter, e.g. 'sh', and guess 'shall' or 'short'. The children then see 's–a'. They might guess 'sand' or 'save'. When the 'i' is shown as well they might think of 'sail' because they expect it to be the 'ai' phoneme.

When the last letter is shown they realise the need to change the pronunciation quite dramatically.
- The words suggested above all work in this way.

Variation

- Use the words to practise oral blending.

Cross-curricular link

English: reading tricky words.

Appendices

APPENDIX 1: PURE SOUNDS

Always use the pure sound of the consonants when you are segmenting words for the children.

Sounds can be 'stopped' or 'continuous':

- 'Stopped' sounds are short and explosive. They are shown as a single-letter sound in the middle column.
- 'Continuous' sounds can be held for as long as you want. They are shown by three of each letter in the middle column.

Remember, 'h' is just a breath – not a noise!

The consonant phoneme	Pronounced ...	... as in ...
b	b	bat
d	d	dog
f	f	fan
g	g	got
h	h	hat
j	j	jar
k	k	kitten
l	lll	let
m	mmm	mat
n	nnn	net
p	p	pen
r	rrr	ran

s	sss	sad
t	t	tap
v	v	van
w	www	win
x	ks	fox
y	yyy	yes
z	zzz	zoo

APPENDIX 2: WATCH OUT!

Watch out for 'w'

W can be linked with a silent **h**, as in:
when, what, where

W can change the vowel sound that follows it, as in:
wasp, want, water
women
wolf

W can be silent, as in:
two
answer

W can be missing altogether, but you can still hear it, as in:
one
once
quick

Watch out for 'ch'

Words written with '**ch**' can be pronounced in one of three ways, dependent upon their origins:
A hard '**ch**', as in *chimney* – Middle English
A soft '**sh**', as in *Charlotte* – French
A '**k**' sound, as in *chemistry* – Greek

Watch out for |l| at the end of words

This can be written as '**le**' or as '**el**', as in:
apple, bottle, table, beetle, castle
label, funnel, barrel

Watch out for the split digraph

The so-called '**magic e**' doesn't always lengthen the vowel sound.
Watch out for:
come, some, have, love

Watch out for the alternative pronunciations for 'ue' and 'ew'

Each of these can be pronounced as /**oo**/ or as /**(y)oo**/, as in:
clue, blue   *grew, blew*
due, cue   *few, stew*

REFERENCES

Official documents

DEE, QCA (1999) *The National Curriculum. Handbook for Primary Teachers in England. Key Stages 1 and 2.*
DfES (2007) *Letters and Sounds. Notes of Guidance for Practitioners and Teachers.* Ref: 00282-2007.
Ofsted (November, 2010) *Reading by Six. How the best schools do it.*

Used or suggested titles for:

Poems

Foster, J. (chosen by) (2003) *Completely Crazy Poems*, London: Collins, imprint of HarperCollins
Lansky, B. (2006) *If Pigs Could Fly ... and Other Deep Thoughts*, Minnetonka, MN: Meadowbrook Press
Waters, F. (1999) *Time for a Rhyme*, London: Orion Children's Books

A selection of nursery rhyme books.

Picture books

Allen, P. (2009) *Grandpa and Thomas and the Green Umbrella*, London: Penguin/Puffin Books
Armitage, R. (2007) *The Lighthouse Keeper's Lunch*, London: Scholastic
Blake, Q. (2010) *Mister Magnolia*, London: Red Fox, Random House Children's Books
Brown, R. (1985) *The Big Sneeze*, London: Andersen Press Ltd
Browne, A. (2010) *Knock, Knock. Who's There?,* London: Picture Puffin
Burningham, J. (1994) *Avocado Baby*, London: Red Fox, Random House Children's Books
Carle, E. (1999) *Do You Want to be my Friend?,* London: Picture Puffins
Carle, E. (2002) *The Very Hungry Caterpillar*, London: Hamish Hamilton
Dahl, R. (2008) *The Enormous Crocodile*, London: Puffin Books
Donaldson, J. (2005) *Chocolate Mousse for Greedy Goose*, London: Macmillan Children's Books
Donaldson, J. (2009) *Toddle Waddle*, London: Macmillan Children's Books

Farjeon, E. (2009) *Cats Sleep Anywhere*, London: Frances Lincoln Publishers Ltd

Finn, I. and Tickle, J. (2000) *The Very Lazy Ladybird*, London: Little Tiger Press

French, V. (2001) *Swallow Journey*, Slough: Zero to Ten Limited

Gravett, E. (2008) *Monkey and Me*, London: Macmillan's Children's Books

Hayes, S. (2003) *This is the Bear and the Picnic Lunch*, London: Walker Books

Hissey, J. (1995) *Little Bear Lost*, London: Hutchinson Children's Books

Hutchins, P. (1978) *Don't Forget the Bacon*, London: Picture Puffins

Inkpen, M. (1991) *The Blue Balloon*, Sevenoaks, Kent: Picture Knight Edition: Hodder and Stoughton Children's Books

Inkpen, M. (2011) *Kipper's Birthday and other stories*, London: Hachette

Inkpen, M. (2006) *Nothing*, London: Hodder Children's Books Children's Books

Kerr, J. (2002) *Mog's Amazing Birthday Caper*, London: Collins Picture Books

Kerr, J. (1973) *The Tiger who Came to Tea*, London: Collins Picture Lions

Martin, J. and Carle, E. (1986) *Brown Bear, Brown Bear, What Can You See?*, London: Picture Lions

McKee, D. (1969) *Two Can, Toucan*, Middlesex: Picture Puffin, Penguin Books

McKee, D. (1990) *Not Now, Bernard*, London: Red Fox, Random House Children's Books

Miller, V. (2001) *Be Gentle*, London: Walker Books Ltd

Munsch, N. (1982) *The Paper Bag Princess*, London: Scholastic Publications

Murphy, J. (1998) *Five Minutes' Peace*, London: Walker Books Ltd

Potter, B. (1987) *The Tale of Mrs Tiggy-Winkle*, London: Frederick Warne

Rayner, C. (2010) *Iris and Isaac*, London: Little Tiger Press, an imprint of Magi Publications

Schaefer, C.L. (2000) *The Copper Tin Cup*, London: Walker Books Ltd

Sendak, M. (1992) *Where the Wild Things Are*, London: Picture Lions, imprint of HarperCollins

Velthuijs, M. (2005) *Frog is Frog*, London: Anderson Press Ltd

Vipont, E. (2000) *The Elephant and the Bad Baby*, London: Picture Puffin

Non·fiction books

Bryant-Mole, K. (1999) *Starting to Measure*, London: Usborne First Learning

Hill, H. (2010) *Harry Hill's Whopping Great Joke Book*, London: Faber and Faber Ltd

Mayes, S. (2004) *The Usborne Book of Dinosaurs*, London: Usborne Publishing

Parker, S. (2008) *100 Things You Should Know About Polar Lands*, Gt Bardfield, Essex: Miles Kelly Publishing

Riley, P. (2001) *Floating and Sinking (Ways into Science)*, London: Franklin Watts

Sims, L. (2002) *The Usborne Book of Castles*, London: Usborne Publishing

Taylor, B. (2001) *Everyday Science: About Your Body*, London: Hodder Children's Books

Art

Mr and Mrs Andrews by Gainsborough
Stanley by David Hockney
Whaam by Roy Lichenstein
The Dance by Matisse
Composition by Mondrian
Poppies by Georgia O'Keeffe
Boy with a Dog by Picasso
Sunday Afternoon on the Island of Grande Jatte by Seurat
Las Meninas by Velazquez
Maurice by Andy Warhol

INDEX OF ACTIVITIES

Activities that focus on phonemes

1. Alliteration

ACTIVITY	FOCUS	PAGE
A counting book	any phoneme	204
A zoo plan	/d/	128
Avocado Baby	/a/	28
Cats with curly tails	/k/	124
Do you know?	any phoneme	242
Five Minutes' Peace	/p/	16
Funny fish	/f/	126
Guesssss	/s/	226
In the garden	/g/	140
Listen before you leap	/l/	228
Little Bear Lost	/b/	32
Monkey and Me	/m/	6
Not Now, Bernard	/n/	14
'Round and round the garden'	/g/	34
Search the library	any phoneme	30
Simon says ...	any phoneme	224

The Copper Tin Cup	any phoneme	68
The Tale of Mrs Tiggy-Winkle	/h/	24
The teacher's pet	/e/	222
The Tiger who Came to Tea (1) & (2)	/t/	10–13
The Very Lazy Ladybird	/l/	18
This is the Bear and the Picnic Lunch	any phoneme	56
Vicky's village shop	/v/	142
What's in Santa's sack?	/r/	130
Yummy yoghurts	/y/	220

2. One spelling for one phoneme

ACTIVITY	FOCUS	PAGE
100 Things You Should Know About Polar Lands	'ze'	78
A bird's eye view	'ar'	146
Castles	'le'	112
Join the gang	'ng'	260
Let's Dance	'ce'	166
Make a bookmark	'sh'	150
Nothing	'th'	58
Owls	'oo'	156

ACTIVITY	FOCUS	PAGE
Something and nothing	'th'	248
Swallow Journey	'our'	110
The Blue Balloon	'oo'	40
The Elephant and the Bad Baby	'ph'	46
Wood and wool	/u/	158

3. Different spellings for one phoneme

ACTIVITY	FOCUS	PAGE
A spell for Josh	/j/	180
A winter's night	'er' 'ir' 'ur' 'w'+'or'	178
Be Gentle	'g' 'ge' 'dge'	82
Crunch, munch	'ch'	280
Full-time	'ch' 'tch'	270
High in the sky	/igh/	282
Iris and Isaac	/igh/	72
Meal times	'ee' 'ea'	264
Mister Magnolia	/oo/	80
Once upon a time	/oa/	172
One morning	/or/	174

Out for a walk	/ow/	188
'Row, row, row your boat'	'oa' 'ow'	76
'The Chocolate Soldier'	'e' 'ea'	66
The playground	/ee/	182
The silver sceptre	's' 'sc' 'ce'	272
The snail trail	/ai/	168
The stormy sea	/sh/	198
The Usborne Book of Dinosaurs	/or/	74
The Venus fly trap	/igh/	190
Underground	/oi/	176
Write a postcard	/ear/	186

4. Range of alternative graphemes and phonemes

ACTIVITY	PAGE
About Your Body	90
Bloo? Blue? Blew?	276
Mog's Amazing Birthday Caper	84
Number rhyme	94
Rhyming colours	274

5. Oral blending and segmenting

ACTIVITY	FOCUS	PAGE
Jim went to the gym	medial vowels	232
Kipper's Birthday	medial vowels	20
Nursery rhyme quiz	medial vowels	22
Nursery rhymes	medial vowels	8
The pottery shop	medial vowels	136
Under my umbrella	medial vowels	26
Frog is Frog	consonant blends	44
Brown Bear, Brown Bear, What Can You See?	range	38
Huff and puff	range	54
Is this my home?	range	256
Phonic wheel	range	160
Sliding sounds	range	132
Spot the odd one out	range	230
Two for one	range	240
Warm up with phonics	range	252
What's in the toy box?	range	284

Activities that focus on words

1. Tricky words

ACTIVITY	FOCUS	PAGE
Could you? Would you?	could, should, would	266
Have fun with tricky words	range	288
The queue	question words	148
The Very Hungry Caterpillar	days of the week	50
What can we do?	he, she, we	258
Where the Wild Things Are	here, there, where	62

2. Compound words

ACTIVITY	PAGE
The Lighthouse Keeper's Lunch	52
Make a new word	318

3. Invented spellings

ACTIVITY	PAGE
Bark and spell!	296
Real or nonsense words	238
Whaam	154

4. Parts of speech

ACTIVITY	FOCUS	PAGE
Poppies	plurals	212
Verb or noun	verb/noun	286

Activities that focus on spelling

1. Suffixes and prefixes

ACTIVITY	FOCUS	PAGE
A pocketful of rye	... 'ful'	114
Floating and sinking	... 'ing'	104
Guess the mime	... 'ly'	306
Make a bridge	... 'er' ... 'est'	210
Mirror, mirror on the wall	... 'est'	96
The Enormous Crocodile	... 'est'	88
Press the rewind button	'un' ...	304
Make it longer	suffixes & prefixes	316
Fireworks (6 activities)	changing tenses	200
The guitar	changing tenses	194

2. Wordplay

ACTIVITY	FOCUS	PAGE
'e' free	individual letters	314
1, 2, 3, 4, go	/oa/	310
All change	segmenting words	312
Bingo	oral blending	320
Guess the word	tricky words	322
Into the woods	names	196
Rainbow games (4 activities)	spelling	234
Strong string	changing letters	250
The Paper Bag Princess	spelling	106
This week's challenge is ...	'ow'	302
What a difference one letter can make!	spelling	300
Work it out	/k/	308

3. Special letters

ACTIVITY	FOCUS	PAGE
Five little bees	/z/	138
'A weird world'	'w'	298
A whole lot of holes	split diagraph 'o-e'	162
Celebration at the space station	'tion'	208
Do You Want to be My Friend?	'w' + 'a'	116
Find the schwa	ə	292
Find the squares	'qu'	152
If Pigs Could Fly ... and Other Deep Thoughts	'ough'	108
Knock, knock. Who's There?	silent k	48
Night in the town	'ch'	170
Nine knights	'n' 'kn' 'gn'	278
Planet X	'x'	134
Starting to Measure	's' as /zh/	92
The case of the missing letter	'w'	206
The Pharaoh's tomb	'mb'	184

4. Rhyme

ACTIVITY	FOCUS	PAGE
Arctic friends	/air/	294
Chocolate Mousse for Greedy Goose	range	70
Don't Forget the Bacon	range	64
'Flo's Toe'	range	42
'I had a little pet'	range	102
Rhythm and rhyme	range	254
Think of a word	/oa/	268
Toddle Waddle	range	98
Two Can, Toucan	range	100
Whoosh! Crash!	/sh/	246